THE UNINHABITABLE EARTH:
LIFE AFTER WARMING

THE UNINHABITABLE EARTH:
LIFE AFTER WARMING

THE UNINHABITABLE EARTH:
LIFE AFTER WARMING

THE UNINHABITABLE EARTH:
LIFE AFTER WARMING

DAVID WALLACE-WELLS

DELACORTE PRESS

Text copyright © 2023 by David Wallace-Wells
Cover art and design by Ray Shappell

All rights reserved. Published in the United States by Delacorte Press, an imprint of
Random House Children's Books, a division of Penguin Random House LLC, New York.

This work is based on *The Uninhabitable Earth: Life After Warming*, originally published in
hardcover by Tim Duggan Books, New York, in 2019 and in paperback by
Tim Duggan Books, in slightly different form, in 2020.

Delacorte Press is a registered trademark and the colophon is a trademark of
Penguin Random House LLC.

Visit us on the Web! GetUnderlined.com

Educators and librarians, for a variety of teaching tools, visit us at
RHTeachersLibrarians.com

Library of Congress Cataloging-in-Publication Data is available upon request.
ISBN 978-0-593-48357-2 (trade pbk.) | ISBN 978-0-593-48355-8 (lib. bdg.) |
ISBN 978-0-593-48356-5 (ebook)

The text of this book is set in 11-point Adobe Caslon Pro.
Interior design by Cathy Bobak
Global warming earth art on part titles by hanohiki/stock.adobe.com

Printed in the United States of America
10 9 8 7 6 5 4 3 2 1
First Edition

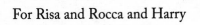

For Risa and Rocca and Harry

CONTENTS

Introduction

You can never really see the future, only imagine it, then try to make sense of the new world when it arrives. Many of the changes happening today that will improve the future have been propelled by youth protesters the world over. This is the strongest reason I wanted an edition of my book for young people.

The edition published by the adult group has been revised and updated, but the core of my research and the facts and details included here will help readers absorb and understand all that is at stake.

The years since initial publication in 2019 have produced waves of scary news about the climate future. But for me, the more important news has been from politics—and it has been remarkably encouraging. Five years ago, almost no one had heard of Greta Thunberg or the Fridays for Future school strikers, Extinction Rebellion, or the Sunrise Movement. There wasn't serious debate about the Green New Deal or the European Green Deal, or even whispers of Fit for 55 or the Inflation Reduction

Act or the Chinese promise to peak emissions by 2030. There were climate-change skeptics in some very conspicuous positions of global power. Hardly any country in the world was talking seriously about eliminating emissions, only reducing them, and many weren't even talking all that seriously about that. Today more than 90 percent of the world's gross domestic product and over 80 percent of global emissions are governed by net-zero pledges of various kinds, each promising thorough decarbonization at historically unprecedented speeds.

Each of these pledges was categorically more serious and ambitious than anything considered politically possible just a few years before. They were also made possible, in large part, by those youth protestors the world over, forcing the issue wherever they could—millions of teenagers and young adults, most without even the power to vote, many of them girls in patriarchal societies and queer in repressive ones, refusing to be silenced and finding a way to make their voices heard all the way up through the world's corridors of powers. And they were heard.

Most of the promises they helped extract were merely notional—empty promises, for now, that might or might not be made real in the years to come. Given how quickly the world must eliminate emissions to avoid the scariest climate consequences, the pledges were also inadequate. But if a skeptic could be forgiven for doubting that those pledges amounted to real progress, a climate optimist could be forgiven for thinking something like the opposite: that everything was moving in the right direction except time, of which we have so little.

That is where we stand today. Where *you* stand—reading this book and contemplating how much is at stake, how much must change, and how quickly.

It can be dizzying to be alive at such a consequential time in human history—intimidating, too. But it is also a gift. A good future is there for the taking—or rather, for the making. Let's not wait.

I

CASCADES

THE WORLD WILL BE WHAT WE MAKE IT—PERHAPS WHAT YOU make it. The timelines are indeed that short.

Consider the speed of change. The earth has experienced five mass extinctions before the one we are living through now, each so complete a wiping of the fossil record that it functioned as an evolutionary reset, the planet's phylogenetic tree first expanding, then collapsing, at intervals, like a lung: 86 percent of all species dead 450 million years ago; 70 million years later, 75 percent; 125 million years later, 96 percent; 50 million years later, 80 percent; 135 million years after that, 75 percent again. All but one of these involved climate change produced by greenhouse gas. The most notorious was 250 million years ago; it began when carbon dioxide warmed the planet by five degrees Celsius, accelerated when that warming triggered the release of methane, another greenhouse gas, and ended with all but a sliver of life on Earth dead. We are currently adding carbon to the atmosphere at a considerably faster rate—by most estimates, at least ten times faster. The rate is one hundred times faster than at any point in human history before the beginning of industrialization. And there is already, right now, fully a third more carbon in the atmosphere than at any point in the last 800,000 years—perhaps in as long as 15 million years. There were no humans then. The oceans were more than a hundred feet higher.

Many perceive global warming as a sort of moral and economic debt, accumulated since the beginning of the Industrial Revolution and now come due after several centuries. In fact, more than half the carbon exhaled into the atmosphere by the burning of fossil fuels has been emitted in just the past three decades. The United Nations established its climate change framework in 1992, building a political consensus out of a scientific consensus and advertising it unmistakably to the world; this means we have now done as much damage to the environment knowingly as we ever managed in ignorance. Global warming may seem like a distended morality tale playing out over several centuries and inflicting a kind of Old Testament retribution on the great-great-grandchildren of those responsible, since it was carbon burning in eighteenth-century England that lit the fuse of everything that has followed. But that is a fable about historical villainy that acquits those of us alive today—unfairly. The majority of the burning has come since the 1994 premiere of *Friends*. A quarter of the damage has been done since Barack Obama was elected president, and Joe Biden vice president, in 2008. Since the end of World War II, the figure is about 90 percent. The story of the industrial world's kamikaze mission is the story of a single lifetime—the planet brought from seeming stability to the brink of catastrophe in the years between a baptism or bar mitzvah and a funeral.

It is the lifetime of many of the scientists who first raised public alarm about climate change, some of whom, incredibly, remain working—that is how rapidly we have arrived at this promontory, staring down the likelihood of three degrees Celsius of warming by the year 2100. Four degrees is possible as well—perhaps more. According to some estimates, that would mean that whole regions of Africa and Australia and the United States, parts of South America north of Patagonia, and Asia south of Siberia would be rendered brutally uncomfortable by direct heat, desertification, and flooding. Certainly, it would make them inhospitable, and many more regions besides. Which means that, if the planet was brought to the brink of climate catastrophe within the lifetime of a single generation, the responsibility to avoid it belongs with a single generation, too. We all also know that second lifetime. It is ours.

I am not an environmentalist and don't even think of myself as a nature person. I've lived my whole life in cities, enjoying gadgets built by industrial supply chains I hardly think twice about. I've never gone camping, not willingly anyway, and while I always thought it was basically a good idea to keep streams clean and air clear, I also always accepted the proposition that there was a trade-off between economic growth and its cost to nature—and figured, well, in most cases I'd probably go for growth. I'm not about to personally slaughter a cow to eat a hamburger, but I'm also not about to go vegan. In these ways—many of them at least—I am like every other American who has spent their life fatally complacent, and willfully deluded, about climate change, which is not just the biggest threat human life on the planet has ever faced but a threat of an entirely different category and scale. That is, the scale of human life itself.

A few years ago, I began collecting stories of climate change, many of them terrifying, gripping, uncanny narratives, with even the most small-scale sagas playing like fables: a group of Arctic scientists trapped when melting ice isolated their research center, on an island populated also by a group of polar bears; a Russian boy killed by anthrax released from a thawing reindeer carcass, which had been trapped in permafrost for many decades. My file of stories grew daily, but very few of the clips, even those drawn from new research published in the most pedigreed scientific journals, seemed to appear in the coverage about climate change the country watched on television and read in its newspapers. In those places, climate change was reported, of course, and even with some tinge of alarm. But the discussion of possible effects was misleadingly narrow, limited almost invariably to the matter of sea-level rise. Just as worrisome, the coverage was sanguine, all things considered. As recently as the 1997 signing of the landmark Kyoto Protocol, two degrees Celsius of global warming was considered the threshold of catastrophe: flooded cities, crippling droughts and heat waves, a planet battered daily by hurricanes and monsoons we used to call "natural disasters" but will soon normalize as simply "bad weather." More recently, the foreign minister of the Marshall Islands offered another name for that level of warming: "genocide."

This is not a book about the science of warming; it is about what warming means to the way we live on this planet. But what does that science say? It is complicated research, because it is built on two layers of uncertainty: what humans will do, mostly in emitting greenhouse gases, but also in how we adapt to the environment we have transformed and how the climate will respond, both through straightforward heating and a variety of more complicated and sometimes contradictory feedback loops. But even shaded by those uncertainty bars, it is also very clear research, in fact terrifyingly clear. The United Nations' Intergovernmental Panel on Climate Change (IPCC) offers the gold-standard assessments of the state of the planet and the likely trajectory for climate change. In its latest report, the IPCC suggested the world was on track for about 3 degrees of warming, bringing the unthinkable collapse of the planet's ice sheets not just into the realm of the real but into the present.

Because these numbers are so small, we tend to trivialize the differences between them—one, two, four, five. Human experience and memory offer no good analogy for how we should think of those thresholds, but, as with world wars or recurrences of cancer, you don't want to see even one.

At two degrees of warming, the ice sheets will likely begin their collapse, 400 million more people could suffer from water scarcity, and major cities in the equatorial band of the planet will become lethally hot in summer. There would be thirty-two times more extreme heat waves in India, and each would last five times as long, exposing ninety-three times more people. This is our best-case scenario.

At three degrees, southern Europe would be in permanent drought, and the average drought in Central America would last nineteen months longer and in the Caribbean twenty-one months longer. In northern Africa, the figure is sixty months longer—five years. The areas burned each year by wildfires would double in the Mediterranean and sextuple, or more, in the United States.

At four degrees, damages from river flooding could grow thirtyfold in Bangladesh, twentyfold in India, and as much as sixtyfold in the United Kingdom. In certain places, six climate-driven natural disasters could strike simultaneously. Conflict and warfare could double.

Even if we pull the planet up short of two degrees by 2100, we will be left with an atmosphere that contains 500 parts per million of carbon—perhaps more. The last time this was the case, sixteen million years ago, the planet was not two degrees warmer; it was somewhere between five and eight, giving the planet about

130 feet of sea-level rise, enough to draw a new American coast-line as far west as I-95. Some of these processes take thousands of years to unfold, but they are also irreversible and therefore effectively permanent. You might hope to simply reverse climate change; you can't. It will outrun all of us.

This is part of what makes climate change what the theorist Timothy Morton calls a "hyperobject"—a conceptual fact so large and complex that, like the internet, it can never be properly comprehended. There are many features of climate change—its size, its scope, its brutality—that alone satisfy this definition; together, they might elevate it into a higher and more incomprehensible conceptual category yet. But time is perhaps the most mind-bending feature, the worst outcomes arriving so long from now that we reflexively discount their reality.

All the paths projected from the present—to two degrees warming, to three, even to four or five—will be carved overwhelmingly by what we choose to do now. There is nothing stopping us from three degrees other than our own will to change course, which we have yet to display. Because the planet is as big as it is, and as ecologically diverse; because humans have proven themselves an adaptable species and will likely continue to adapt to outmaneuver a lethal threat; and because the devastating effects of warming will soon become too extreme to ignore or deny, if they haven't already; because of all that, it is unlikely that climate change will render the planet truly uninhabitable. But if we do nothing about carbon emissions, if the next thirty years of industrial activity trace the same arc upward as the last thirty years have, whole regions will become unlivable by any standard we have today, as soon as the end of this century.

What this means is that we have not at all arrived at a new equilibrium. It is more like we've taken one step out on the plank of a pirate ship. Perhaps because of the exhausting false debate about whether climate change is "real," too many of us have developed a misleading impression of its effects. Global warming is not "yes" or "no," nor is it "today's weather forever" or "doomsday tomorrow." It is a function that gets worse over time as long as we continue to produce greenhouse gas. And so the experience of life in a climate transformed by human activity is not just a matter of stepping from one stable ecosystem into another, somewhat worse one, no matter how degraded or destructive the transformed climate is. The effects will grow and build as the planet continues to warm: from 1 degree to 1.5 to almost certainly 2 degrees and beyond. The last few years of climate disasters may look like about as much as the planet can take. In fact, we are only just entering our brave new world, one that collapses below us as soon as we set foot on it. For climate change isn't something happening here or there but everywhere, and all at once. And unless we choose to halt it, it will never stop.

Just how completely the world below our feet will become unknown to us is not yet clear, and how we register its transformation remains an open question. One legacy of the environmentalist creed that long prized the natural world as an otherworldly retreat is that we see its degradation as a sequestered story, unfolding separately from our own modern lives.

In just the last forty years, according to the World Wildlife Fund, more than half the world's vertebrate animals have died; in just the last twenty-five years, one study of German nature preserves found, the flying insect population declined by three-quarters. Species individuated over millions of years of evolution, but now forced together by climate change, they have begun to mate with one another for the first time, producing a whole new class of hybrid species: the pizzly bear, the coywolf. The zoos are already natural history museums, the children's books already out-of-date. Little of this book, however, is about "nature" per se, and none of it concerns the tragic fate of the planet's animals, which has been written about so elegantly and poetically by others that, like our sea-level myopia, it threatens to occlude our picture of what global warming means for us, the human animal. Until now, it seems to have been easier for us to empathize with the climate plight of other species than with our own, perhaps because we have such a hard time acknowledging or understanding our own responsibility and complicity in the changes now unfolding, and such an easier time evaluating the morally simpler calculus of pure victimhood.

That we know global warming is our doing should be a comfort, not a cause for despair, however incomprehensively large and complicated we find the processes that have brought it into being. That we know we are, ourselves, responsible for all its punishing effects should be empowering, and not just perversely so. Global warming is, after all, a human invention. And the flip side of our real-time guilt is that we remain in command. No matter how out of control the climate system seems—with its roiling typhoons, unprecedented famines and heat waves, refugee crises and climate conflicts—we are all its authors.

Some, like our oil companies and their political patrons, are more prolific authors than others. Each of us imposes some suffering on our future selves every time we flip on a light switch, buy a plane ticket, or fail to vote. Now we all share the responsibility to write the next act. We found a way to engineer devastation, and we can find a way to engineer our way out of it—or, rather, engineer our way toward a degraded muddle, but one that nevertheless extends the promise of new generations finding their own way forward, perhaps toward some brighter environmental future.

Since I first began writing about warming, I've often been asked whether I see any reason for optimism. The thing is, I *am* optimistic. Given the prospect that humans could engineer a climate that is 4 degrees warmer over the course of the next several centuries—a degraded muddle counts, for me, as an encouraging future. Yes, warming of 2 or 2.5 degrees would probably unleash enormous amounts of needless suffering, distributed cruelly to those least able to protect themselves, beyond anything that humans have ever experienced through many millennia of strain and strife and all-out war. But also quite a bit better than where we are currently headed. Given the basic mystery of the future, better than that is still possible too—bringing the planet closer to a state we would today regard as merely grim rather than apocalyptic.

That is the cause of hope—no matter how grim the future, the future is never scripted. Many avenues are open—wide open, if we are not too lazy and too blinkered and too selfish to embark upon them.

ELEMENTS OF CHAOS

Heat Death

HUMANS, LIKE ALL MAMMALS, ARE HEAT ENGINES; SURVIVING means having to continually cool off, as panting dogs do. For that, the temperature needs to be low enough for the air to act as a kind of refrigerant, drawing heat off the skin so the engine can keep pumping. At seven degrees Celsius of warming, that would become impossible in portions of the planet's equatorial band, and especially the tropics, where humidity adds to the problem. And the effect would be fast: after a few hours, a human body would be cooked to death from both inside and out.

At just five degrees, according to some calculations, whole parts of the globe would be literally unsurvivable for humans. These calculations are just crude models of the planetary heat experiment we will be running in the decades to come, and there are some reasons to be cautious in extrapolating their lessons.

But at just two degrees, it is expected that cities now home to millions, across India and the Middle East, would become so hot that stepping outside in summer would be a lethal risk to many who live there.

With direct heat, the key factor is something called "wet-bulb temperature," which also measures humidity in a combined method as home-laboratory kit as it sounds: the temperature is registered on a thermometer wrapped in a damp sock as it's swung around in the air. At present, most regions reach a wet-bulb maximum of 26 or 27 degrees Celsius; the true red line for habitability is 35 degrees, beyond which humans begin simply dying from the heat. That leaves a gap of 8 degrees. What is called "heat stress" comes much sooner.

Actually, we're there already. Since 1980, the planet has experienced a fiftyfold increase in the number of dangerous heat waves; a bigger increase is to come. The five warmest summers in Europe since 1500 have all occurred since 2002, and eventually, the IPCC warns, simply working outdoors at that time of year will be unhealthy for parts of the globe. Even if we meet the Paris goals, cities like Karachi and Kolkata will annually encounter deadly heat waves like those that crippled them in 2015, when heat killed thousands in India and Pakistan. At four degrees, the deadly European heat wave of 2003, which killed as many as 2,000 people a day, will be a normal summer. Then, it was one of the worst weather events in Continental history, killing 35,000 Europeans, including 14,000 French; perversely, the infirm fared relatively well, William Langewiesche has written, most of them watched over in the nursing homes and hospitals of those well-off countries, and it was the comparatively healthy elderly who accounted for most of the dead, many left behind by vacationing families escaping the heat, with some corpses rotting for weeks before the families returned.

We had heat waves back at the end of the twentieth century, of course—deadly ones; in 1998, the Indian summer killed 2,500. More recently, temperature spikes have gotten hotter. In 2010, 55,000 died in a Russian heat wave that killed 700 people in Moscow each day. In 2016, in the midst of a heat wave that baked the Middle East for several months, temperatures in Iraq broke 100 degrees Fahrenheit in May, 110 in June, and 120 in July, with temperatures most days dipping below 100 only at night. In 2018, the hottest temperature likely ever recorded in April was registered in southeast Pakistan. In India, a single day over 95 degrees Fahrenheit increases annual mortality rates by three-quarters of a percent; in 2016, a string of days topped 120—in May. In Saudi Arabia, where summer temperatures often approach that mark, 700,000 barrels of oil are burned each day in the summer, mostly to power the nation's air-conditioning.

That can help with the heat, of course, but air conditioners and fans already account for fully 10 percent of global electricity consumption. Demand is expected to triple, or perhaps quadruple, by 2050; according to one estimate, the world will be adding 700 million AC units by just 2030. Another study suggests that by 2050 there will be, around the world, more than nine billion cooling appliances of various kinds. But, the climate-controlled malls of the Arab emirates aside, it is not remotely economical, let alone "green," to wholesale air-condition all the hottest parts of the planet, many of them also the poorest. And indeed, the crisis will be most dramatic across the Middle East and Persian Gulf, where in 2015 the heat index registered temperatures as high as 163 degrees Fahrenheit. As soon as several decades from now, the hajj will become physically impossible for many of the two million Muslims who currently make the pilgrimage to Mecca each year.

It is not just the hajj, and it is not just Mecca. In the sugarcane region of El Salvador, as much as one-fifth of the population— including over a quarter of the men—has chronic kidney disease, the presumed result of dehydration from working the fields they were able to comfortably harvest as recently as two decades ago. With dialysis, which is expensive, those with kidney failure can expect to live five years; without it, life expectancy is measured in weeks. Of course, heat stress promises to assail us in places other than our kidneys, too. As I type that sentence, in the California desert in mid-June, it is 121 degrees outside my door. It is not a record high.

How much hotter will it get? The menace of climate change is a mercurial one; uncertainty makes it a shape-shifting threat. When will the planet warm by two degrees, and when by three? How much sea-level rise will be here by 2030, by 2050, by 2100, as our children are leaving the earth to their children and grand-children? Which cities will flood, which forests will dry out, which breadbaskets will become husks? That uncertainty is among the most momentous metanarratives that climate change will bring to our culture over the next decades. But while there are a few things science does not know about how the climate system will respond to all the carbon we've pumped into the air, the uncertainty of what will happen—that haunting uncertainty—emerges not from scientific ignorance but, overwhelmingly, from the open question of how we respond. Because when it comes to global warming, the key input is a mystery: What will we do?

The lessons there are unfortunately bleak. Three-quarters of a century since global warming was first recognized as a problem, we have made no meaningful adjustment to our production or consumption of energy to account for it and protect ourselves. For far too long, casual climate observers have watched scientists draw pathways to a stable climate and concluded that the world would adapt accordingly; instead, the world has done too little, as though those pathways would implement themselves. Market forces have delivered cheaper and more widely available green energy, but the same market forces have absorbed those innovations, which is to say profited from them, while continuing to grow emissions. In recent years, some of those trends have finally—decades too late—taken an encouraging turn, with renewables growing as a share of total global energy. But bringing global emissions to a sort of plateau is only the very beginning of the battle—a carbon peak means only that we have successfully managed to avoid doing more damage to the planet's future than in any previous year in human history. From there, it is a very long way down to zero emissions, where we need to be. During the recent spasm of climate enthusiasm among world leaders, politics has produced gestures of tremendous global solidarity and cooperation, then discarded those promises immediately. It has become commonplace among climate activists to say that we have, today, all the tools we need to avoid catastrophic climate change—even major climate change. It is also true. But political will is not some trivial ingredient always at hand.

Cities, where the world will overwhelmingly live in the near future, only magnify the problem of high temperature. Asphalt and concrete and everything else that makes a city dense, including human flesh, absorb ambient heat, essentially storing it for a time like a slow-release poison pill; this is especially problematic because, in a heat wave, nightly reprieves are vital, allowing bodies to recover. When those reprieves are shorter, and shallower, flesh simply continues to simmer. In fact, the concrete and asphalt of cities absorb so much heat during the day that when it is released, at night, it can raise the local temperature as much as 22 degrees Fahrenheit, turning what could be bearably hot days into deadly ones—as in the Chicago heat wave of 1995, which killed 739 people, the direct-heat effects compounded by broken public health infrastructure. That commonly cited figure reflects only immediate deaths; of the many thousands more who visited hospitals during the heat wave, almost half died within the year. Others suffered permanent brain damage. Scientists call this the "heat island" effect—each city is its own enclosed space, and hotter the more crowded it is.

Of course, the world is rapidly urbanizing, with the United Nations estimating that two-thirds of the global population will live in cities by 2050—2.5 billion new urbanites, by that count. For a century or more, the city has seemed like a vision of the future to much of the world, which keeps inventing new scales of metropolis: bigger than 5 million people, bigger than 10, bigger than 20. Climate change won't likely slow that pattern by much, but it will make the great migrations it reflects more perilous, with many millions of the world's ambitious flooding into cities whose calendars are dotted with days of deadly heat, gathering in those new megalopolises like moths to a flame.

In theory, climate change could even reverse those migrations, perhaps more totally than crime did in many American cities in the last century, turning urban populations in certain parts of the world outward as the cities themselves become unbearable. In the heat, roads in cities will melt and train tracks will buckle—this is actually happening already, but the impacts will mushroom in the decades ahead. Currently, there are 354 major cities with average maximum summertime temperatures of 95 degrees Fahrenheit or higher. By 2050, that list could grow to 970, and the number of people living in those cities and exposed to that deadly heat could grow eightfold, to 1.6 billion. In the United States alone, 70,000 workers have been seriously injured by heat since 1992, and by 2050, 255,000 are expected to die globally from direct heat effects. Already, as many as 1 billion are at risk for heat stress worldwide, and a third of the world's population is subject to deadly heat waves at least twenty days each year; by 2100, that third will grow to half, even if we manage to pull up short of two degrees. If we don't, the number could climb to three-quarters.

In the United States, heat stroke has a pathetic reputation— a plague you learn about from summer camp, like swimming cramps. But heat death is among the cruelest punishments to a human body, just as painful and disorienting as hypothermia. First comes "heat exhaustion," mostly a mark of dehydration: profuse sweating, nausea, headache. After a certain point, though, water won't help, your core temperature rising as your body sends blood outward to the skin, hoping desperately to cool it down. The skin often reddens; internal organs begin to fail. Eventually, you could stop sweating. The brain, too, stops working properly, and sometimes, after a period of agitation and combativeness, the episode is punctuated with a lethal heart attack. "When it comes to extreme heat," Langewiesche has written, "you can no more escape the conditions than you can shed your skin."

Hunger

CLIMATES DIFFER AND PLANTS VARY, BUT A BASIC RULE OF thumb for staple cereal crops grown at optimal temperature is that for every degree of warming, yields decline by 10 percent. Some estimates run higher. Which means that if the planet is four degrees warmer at the end of the century, when projections suggest we may have as many as 50 percent more people to feed, we may also have 50 percent less grain to give them. And proteins are worse: it takes eight pounds of grain to produce just a single pound of hamburger meat, butchered from a cow that spent its life warming the planet with methane burps.

Globally, grain accounts for about 40 percent of the human diet; when you add soybeans and corn, you get up to two-thirds of all human calories. Overall, the United Nations estimates that the planet will need nearly twice as much food in 2050 as it does today—and although this is a speculative figure, it's not a bad one. Pollyannaish plant physiologists will point out that the cereal-crop math applies only to those regions already at peak growing temperature, and they are right—theoretically, a warmer climate will make it easier to grow wheat in Greenland. But as a path-breaking paper by Rosamond Naylor and David Battisti pointed out, the tropics are already too hot to efficiently grow grain, and those places where grain is produced today are already at optimal growing temperature—which means even a small warming will push them down a slope of declining productivity. The same, broadly speaking, is true for corn. At four degrees of warming, corn yields in the United States, the world's top producer of maize, are expected to drop by almost half. Predicted declines are not quite as dramatic in the next three biggest producers—China, Argentina, Brazil—but in each case the country would lose at least a fifth of its productivity.

A decade ago, climatologists might have told you that although direct heat undermined plant growth, the extra carbon in the atmosphere would have the opposite effect—a kind of airborne fertilizer. The effect is strongest on weeds, though, and does not seem to hold for grain. And at higher concentrations of carbon, plants grow thicker leaves, which sounds innocuous. But thicker leaves are worse at absorbing CO_2, an effect that means, by the end of the century, as much as 6.39 billion additional tons of it in the atmosphere each year.

Beyond carbon, climate change means staple crops are doing

battle with more insects—their increased activity could cut yields an additional 2 to 4 percent—as well as fungus and disease, not to mention flooding. Some crops, like sorghum, are a bit more robust, but even in those regions where such alternatives have been a staple, their production has diminished recently; and while grain breeders have some hope that they can produce more-heat-tolerant strains, they've been trying for decades without success. The world's natural wheat belt is moving poleward by about 160 miles each decade, but you can't easily move croplands north a few hundred miles—and not just because it's difficult to suddenly clear the land occupied now by towns, highways, office parks, and industrial installations. Yields in places like remote areas of Canada and Russia, even if they warmed by a few degrees, would be limited by the quality of soil there, since it takes many centuries for the planet to produce optimally fertile dirt. The lands that are fertile are the ones we are already using, and the climate is changing much too fast to wait for the northern soil to catch up. That soil, believe it or not, is literally disappearing—75 billion tons of soil lost each year. In the United States, the rate of erosion is ten times higher than the natural replenishment rate; in China and India, it is thirty to forty times faster.

Even when we try to adapt, we move too slowly. Economist Richard Hornbeck specializes in the history of the American Dust Bowl; he says that farmers of that era could conceivably have adapted to the changing climate of their time by cultivating different crops. But they didn't, lacking credit to make the necessary investments—and were therefore unable to shake inertia and ritual and the rootedness of identity. So instead, the crops died out, in cascading waves crashing through whole American states and all the people living in them.

As it happens, a similar transformation is unfolding in the American West right now. In 1879, the naturalist John Wesley Powell, who spent his downtime as a soldier during the Battle of Vicksburg studying the rocks that filled the Union trenches, divined a natural boundary running due north along the 100th meridian. It separated the humid—and therefore cultivable—natural farmland of what became the Midwest from the arid, spectacular, but less farmable land of the true West. The divide runs through Texas, Oklahoma, Kansas, Nebraska, and the Dakotas, and stretches south into Mexico and north into Manitoba, Canada, separating more densely populated communities full of large farms from sparser, open land that was never truly made valuable by agriculture. Since just 1980, that boundary has moved fully 140 miles east, almost to the 98th meridian, drying up hundreds of thousands of square miles of farmland in the process.

Drought may be an even bigger problem for food production than heat, with some of the world's most arable land turning quickly to desert. At 2 degrees of warming, droughts will wallop the Mediterranean and much of India, and corn and sorghum all around the world will suffer, straining global food supply. At 2.5 degrees, thanks mostly to drought, the world could enter a global food deficit—needing more calories than the planet can produce. At 3 degrees, there would be further drought—in Central America, Pakistan, the western United States, and Australia. At 5 degrees, the whole earth would be wrapped in what the environmentalist Mark Lynas calls "two globe-girdling belts of perennial drought."

Precipitation is notoriously hard to model in detail, yet predictions for later this century are basically unanimous: both unprecedented droughts and unprecedented flood-producing rains. By 2080, without dramatic reductions in emissions, southern Europe will be in permanent extreme drought, much worse than the American Dust Bowl ever was. The same will be true in Iraq and Syria and much of the rest of the Middle East; some of the most densely populated parts of Australia, Africa, and South America; and the breadbasket regions of China. As for the original Dust Bowl: the droughts in the American plains and Southwest would not just be worse than in the 1930s, a 2015 NASA study predicted, but worse than any droughts in a thousand years—and that includes those that struck between 1100 and 1300, which dried up all the rivers east of the Sierra Nevada mountains and may have been responsible for the death of the Anasazi civilization.

Remember, even with the remarkable gains of the last decades, we do not presently live in a world without hunger. Far from it: most estimates put the number of undernourished at 800 million globally, with as many as 100 million hungry because of climate shocks. What is called "hidden hunger"—micronutrient and dietary deficiencies—is considerably higher, affecting well over 1 billion people.

Drowning

IN *THE WATER WILL COME,* JEFF GOODELL RUNS THROUGH just a few of the monuments—indeed, in some cases, whole cultures—that will be transformed into underwater relics, like sunken ships, this century: any beach you've ever visited; Facebook's headquarters, the Kennedy Space Center, and the United States's largest naval base, in Norfolk, Virginia; the entire nations of the Maldives and the Marshall Islands; most of Bangladesh, including all the mangrove forests that have been the kingdom of Bengal tigers for millennia; all of Miami Beach and much of the South Florida paradise engineered out of marsh and swamp and sandbar by rabid real-estate speculators less than a century ago; Saint Mark's Basilica in Venice, today nearly a thousand years old; Venice Beach and Santa Monica in Los Angeles; the White House at 1600 Pennsylvania Avenue, as well as Donald Trump's

"Winter White House" at Mar-a-Lago, Richard Nixon's in Key Biscayne, and the original, Harry Truman's, in Key West. This is a very partial list. By 2100, if we do not halt emissions, as much as 5 percent of the world's population will be flooded every single year. Jakarta is one of the world's fastest-growing cities, today home to ten million; thanks to flooding and literal sinking, it could be entirely underwater as soon as 2050. Already, China is evacuating hundreds of thousands every summer to keep them out of the range of flooding in the Pearl River Delta.

What would be submerged by these floods are not just the homes of those who flee—perhaps hundreds of millions of climate refugees seeking help in a world incapable, at this point, of accommodating the needs of only a few million—but communities, schools, shopping districts, farmlands, office buildings, and high-rises, regional cultures so sprawling that just a few centuries ago we might have remembered them as empires unto themselves, now suddenly underwater museums showcasing the way of life in the one or two centuries when humans, rather than keeping their safe distance, rushed to build up at the coastline.

Much of the infrastructure of the internet, one study showed, could be drowned by sea-level rise in fewer than two decades; and most of the smartphones we use to navigate it are today manufactured in Shenzhen, which, sitting right in the Pearl River Delta, is likely to be flooded soon as well. In 2018, the Union of Concerned Scientists found that nearly 311,000 homes in the United States would be at risk of chronic inundation by 2045—a time span, as they pointed out, no longer than a mortgage. By 2100, the number would be more than 2.4 million properties, or $1 trillion worth of American real estate at risk.

But the flooding wouldn't stop at the end of the century, since sea-level rise would continue for millennia and ultimately produce, even in that optimistic two-degree scenario, oceans almost twenty feet (six meters) higher. What would that look like? The planet would lose about 444,000 square miles of land, where about 375 million people live today—a quarter of them in China. In fact, the twenty cities most affected by such sea-level rise are all Asian megalopolises—among them Shanghai, Hong Kong, Mumbai, and Kolkata. China may well continue its geopolitical ascent in the coming decades, but it will do so while fighting back the ocean—perhaps one reason it is already so focused on establishing control over the South China Sea.

Nearly two-thirds of the world's major cities are on the coast—not to mention its power plants, ports, navy bases, farmlands, fisheries, river deltas, marshlands, and rice paddies—and even those above ten feet will flood much more easily, and much more regularly, if the water gets that high. Already, flooding has quadrupled since 1980, according to the European Academies' Science Advisory Council, and doubled since just 2004. Even under an "intermediate low" sea-level-rise scenario, by 2100, high-tide flooding could hit the East Coast of the United States "every other day."

We haven't even gotten to inland flooding—when rivers run

over, swollen by deluges of rain or storm surges channeled down-stream from the sea. Between 1995 and 2015, this affected 2.3 billion and killed 157,000 around the world. At just 1.5 degrees Celsius of warming, flood damage would increase by between 160 and 240 percent; at 2 degrees, the death toll from flooding would be 50 percent higher than today. In the United States, one recent model suggested that FEMA's recent projections of flood risk were off by a factor of three, and that more than 40 million Americans were at risk of catastrophic inundation.

Keep in mind that these effects will come to pass even with a radical reduction of emissions. Without flood adaptation measures, large swaths of northern Europe and the whole eastern half of the United States will be affected by at least ten times as many floods. In large parts of India, Bangladesh, and Southeast Asia, where flooding is today catastrophically common, the multiplier could be just as high—and the baseline is already so elevated that it annually produces humanitarian crises on a scale we like to think we would not forget for generations.

Instead, we forget them immediately.

To what degree we will be able to adapt to new coastlines is primarily a matter of just how fast the water rises. Our understanding of that timeline has been evolving disconcertingly fast. When the Paris Agreement was drafted, those writing it were sure that the Antarctic ice sheets would remain stable even as the planet warmed several degrees; they expected that oceans could rise, at most, only three feet by the end of the century. That was in 2015. The same year, NASA found that this expectation was hopelessly complacent, suggesting three feet was not a maximum but in fact a minimum. In 2017, the National Oceanic and Atmospheric Administration (NOAA) suggested eight feet was possible—still just in this century. On the East Coast, scientists have already introduced a new term, "sunny day flooding"—when high tide alone, aided by no additional rainstorm, inundates a town.

In 2018, a major study found things accelerating faster still, with the melt rate of the Antarctic ice sheet tripling in the past decade alone. From 1992 to 1997, the sheet lost, on average, 49 billion tons of ice each year; from 2012 to 2017, it was 219 billion. In 2016, climate scientist James Hansen had suggested sea level could rise several feet during fifty years if ice melt doubled every decade; the 2018 paper, keep in mind, registers a tripling, and in the space of only five years. Since the 1950s, the continent has lost 13,000 square miles from its ice shelf; experts say its ultimate fate will probably be determined by what human action is taken in the next decade.

All climate change is governed by uncertainty, mostly the uncertainty of human action—what action will be taken, and when, to avert or forestall the dramatic transformation of life on the planet, which will unfold in the absence of dramatic intervention. Each of our projections, from the most blasé to the most extreme, comes wrapped in doubt—the result of so many estimates and so many assumptions that it would be foolish to take any of them, so to speak, to the bank.

But sea-level rise is different, because on top of the basic mystery of human response, it layers much more epistemological ignorance than governs any other aspect of climate change science, save perhaps the question of cloud formation. When water warms, it expands: this we know. But the breaking-up of ice represents almost an entirely new physics, never before observed in human history, and therefore only poorly understood.

One study suggests that the Greenland ice sheet could reach a tipping point at just 1.2 degrees of global warming. (We are nearing that temperature level today, already at 1.1 degrees.) Melting that ice sheet alone would, over centuries, raise sea levels almost twenty feet (six meters), eventually drowning Miami and Manhattan and London and Shanghai and Bangkok and Mumbai. And while high-end emissions trajectories warm the planet by just over 4 degrees by 2100, temperature changes are unevenly distributed around the planet, so they threaten to warm the Arctic by 13 degrees.

In 2014, we learned that the West Antarctic and Greenland ice sheets were even more vulnerable to melting than scientists anticipated—in fact, the West Antarctic sheet had already passed a tipping point of collapse, more than doubling its rate of ice loss in only five years. The same had happened in Greenland, where the ice sheet is now losing almost a billion tons of ice every single day. The two sheets contain enough ice to raise global sea levels

ten to twenty feet—each. In 2017, it was revealed that two glaciers in the East Antarctic sheet were also losing ice at an alarming rate—eighteen billion tons of ice each year, enough to cover
New Jersey in three feet of ice. If both glaciers go, scientists expect ultimately an additional 16 feet of water. In total, the two
Antarctic ice sheets could raise sea level by 200 feet; in many parts
of the world, the shoreline would move by many miles.

Wildfire

THE TIME BETWEEN THANKSGIVING AND CHRISTMAS IS MEANT to be, in Southern California, the start of rainy season. Not in 2017. The Thomas Fire, the worst of those that roiled the region that fall, grew 50,000 acres in one day, eventually burning 440 square miles and forcing the evacuations of more than 100,000 Californians. A week after it was sparked, it remained merely "15% contained."

"The city burning is Los Angeles's deepest image of itself," Joan Didion wrote in "Los Angeles Notebook," collected in *Slouching Towards Bethlehem,* published in 1968. But the cultural impression is apparently not all that deep, since the fires that broke out in the fall of 2017 produced, in headlines and on television and via text messages, an astonished refrain of the adjectives "unthinkable," "unprecedented," and "unimaginable." Didion was writing about the fires that had swept through Malibu in 1956, Bel Air in 1961, Santa Barbara in 1964, and Watts in 1965; she updated her list in 1989 with "Fire Season," in which she described the fires of 1968, 1970, 1975, 1978, 1979, 1980, and 1982: "Since 1919, when the county began keeping records of its fires, some areas have burned eight times."

But all fires, of course, are not equal. Five of the twenty worst fires in California history hit the state in the fall of 2017, a year in which over nine thousand separate ones broke out, burning through more than 1,240,000 acres—nearly two thousand square miles made soot.

That October, in Northern California, 172 fires broke out in just two days—devastation so cruel and sweeping that two different accounts were published in two different local newspapers of two different aging couples taking desperate cover in pools as the fires swallowed their homes. One couple survived, emerging after six excruciating hours to find their house transformed into an ash monument; in the other account, it was only the husband who emerged, his wife of fifty-five years having died in his arms. As Americans traded horror stories in the aftermath of those fires, they could be forgiven for mixing up the stories, or being confused; that climate terror could be so general as to provide variations on such a theme had seemed, as recently as that September, impossible to believe.

The following year offered another variation. In the summer of 2018, the fires were fewer in number, totaling only six thousand. But just one, made up of a whole network of fires together called the Mendocino Complex, burned almost half a million acres alone. In total, more than two thousand square miles in the state turned to flame, and smoke blanketed almost half the country. Things were worse to the north, in British Columbia, where more than three million acres burned, producing smoke that would—if it followed the pattern of previous Canadian plumes—travel across the Atlantic to Europe. Then, in November came the Woolsey Fire, which forced the evacuation of 170,000, and the Camp Fire, which was somehow worse, burning through more than two hundred square miles and incinerating an entire town so quickly that the evacuees, 50,000 of them, found themselves sprinting past exploding cars, their sneakers melting to the asphalt as they ran. It was the deadliest fire in California history, a record that had been set almost a century before, by the Griffith Park Fire of 1933.

As a whole, the year 2018 set a new record for acres burned in California. The fires in 2020 more than doubled it.

Two big forces conspire to prevent us from normalizing fires like these, though neither is exactly a cause for celebration. The first is that extreme weather won't let us, since it won't stabilize—so that even within a decade, it's a fair bet that these fires, which now occupy the nightmares of every Californian, will be thought of as the "old normal." The good old days.

The second force is also contained in the story of the wild-fires: the way climate change is finally striking close to home. Some quite special homes. The California fires of 2017 burned the state's wine crop, blowtorched million-dollar vacation properties, and threatened both the Getty Museum and Rupert Murdoch's Bel Air estate. There may not be two better symbols of the imperiousness of American money than those two structures. Nearby, the sunshiny children's fantasia of Disneyland was quickly canopied, as the fires began to encroach, by an eerily apocalyptic orange sky. On local golf courses, the West Coast's wealthy still showed up for their tee times, swinging their clubs just yards from blazing fires, caught in photographs that could not have been more perfectly staged to skewer the country's indifferent plutocracy. The following year, Americans watched the Kardashians evacuate via Instagram stories, then read about the private firefighting forces they employed, the rest of the state reliant on conscripted convicts earning as little as a dollar a day.

By accidents of geography and by the force of its wealth, the United States has, to this point, been mostly protected from the devastation climate change has already visited on parts of the less-developed world—mostly. The fact that warming is now hitting our wealthiest citizens is not just an opportunity for ugly bursts of liberal schadenfreude; it is also a sign of just how hard, and how indiscriminately, it is hitting. All of a sudden, it's getting a lot harder to protect against what's coming.

What is coming? Much more fire, much more often, burning much more land. Over the last five decades, the wildfire season in the western United States has already grown by two and a half months; of the ten years with the most wildfire activity on record, nine have occurred since 2000. Globally, since just 1979, the season has grown by nearly 20 percent, and American wildfires now burn twice as much land as they did as recently as 1970. By 2050, destruction from wildfires is expected to double again, and in some places within the United States, the area burned could grow fivefold. For every additional degree of global warming, it could quadruple. What this means is that at three degrees of warming, our likely benchmark for the end of the century, the United States might be dealing with sixteen times more devastation from fire than we are today, when in a single year ten million acres were burned. At four degrees of warming, the fire season would be four times worse still. The California fire captain believes the term is already outdated: "We don't even call it fire season anymore," he said in 2017. "Take the 'season' out—it's year-round."

But wildfires are not an American affliction; they are a global pandemic. In icy Greenland, fires in 2017 appeared to burn ten times more area than in 2014; and in Sweden, in 2018, forests in the Arctic Circle went up in flames. Fires that far north may seem innocuous, relatively speaking, since there are not so many people up there. But they are increasing more rapidly than fires in lower latitudes, and they concern climate scientists greatly: the soot and ash they give off can land on and blacken ice sheets, which then absorb more of the sun's rays and melt more quickly. Another Arctic fire broke out on the Russia-Finland border in 2018, and smoke from Siberian fires that summer reached all the way to the mainland United States. The same month, the twenty-first century's second-deadliest wildfire had swept through the Greek seaside, killing ninety-nine. At one resort, dozens of guests tried to escape the flames by descending a narrow stone staircase into the Aegean Sea, only to be engulfed along the way, dying literally in each other's arms.

The effects of these fires are not linear or neatly additive. It might be more accurate to say that they initiate a new set of biological cycles. Scientists warn that, even as California is baked into brush by a drier future, making inevitable more and more damaging fires, the probability of unprecedented-seeming rainfalls will grow, too—as much as a threefold increase of events like that which produced the state's Great Flood of 1862. And mudslides are among the clearest illustrations of what new horrors that heralds; in Santa Barbara that January, the town's low-lying homes were pounded by the mountains' detritus cascading down the hillside toward the ocean in an endless brown river. One father, in a panic, put his young children up on his kitchen's marble countertop, thinking it the strongest feature of the house, then watched as a rolling boulder smashed through the bedroom where the children had been just moments before. One kindergartner who didn't make it was found close to two miles from his home, in a gulley traced by train tracks close to the waterfront, having been carried there, presumably, on a continuous wave of mud. Two miles.

When trees die—by natural processes, by fire, at the hands of humans—they release into the atmosphere the carbon stored within them, sometimes for as long as centuries. In this way, they are like coal. Which is why the effect of wildfires on emissions is among the most feared climate feedback loops—that the world's forests, which have typically been carbon sinks, would become carbon sources, unleashing all that stored gas. The impact can be especially dramatic when the fires ravage forests arising out of peat. Peatland fires in Indonesia in 1997, for instance, released up to 2.6 billion tons of carbon—40 percent of the average annual global emissions level. The catastrophic Australia fires that began in 2019, burning for months, doubled that country's emissions. And more burning only means more warming only means more burning. In California, a single wildfire can entirely eliminate the emissions gains made that year by all the state's aggressive environmental policies. Fires of that scale happen now every year. In this way, they make a mockery of the technocratic, idealist approach to emissions reduction. In the Amazon, which in 2010 suffered its second "hundred-year drought" in the space of five years, 100,000 fires were found to be burning in 2017. In 2021, there was more carbon emitted from global forest fire than from any country but the United States and China, the world's two largest emitters.

Globally, deforestation accounts for about 12 percent of carbon emissions, and forest fires produce as much as 25 percent. The ability of forest soils to absorb methane has fallen by 77 percent in just three decades, and some of those studying the rate of tropical deforestation believe it could deliver an additional 1.5 degrees Celsius of global warming even if fossil fuel emissions immediately ceased.

Historically, the emissions rate from deforestation was even higher, with the clearing of woods and flattening of forests causing 30 percent of emissions from 1861 to 2000; until 1980, deforestation played a greater role in increases of hottest-day records than did direct greenhouse-gas emissions. There is a public health impact as well: every square kilometer of deforestation produces twenty-seven additional cases of malaria, thanks to "vector proliferation"—when the trees are cleared out, the bugs move in.

Freshwater Drain

SEVENTY-ONE PERCENT OF THE PLANET IS COVERED IN WATER. Barely more than 2 percent of that water is fresh, and only 1 percent of that water, at most, is accessible, with the rest trapped mostly in glaciers. Which means, in essence, as *National Geographic* has calculated, only 0.007 percent of the planet's water is available to fuel and feed its seven billion people.

Think of freshwater shortages and you probably feel an itch in your throat, yet hydration is just a sliver of what we need water for. Globally, between 70 and 80 percent of fresh water is used for food production and agriculture, with an additional 10 to 20 percent set aside for industry. And the crisis is not principally driven by climate change—that 0.007 percent should be, believe it or not, plenty, not just for the seven billion of us here but for as many as nine billion, perhaps even a bit more. Of course, we are likely heading north of nine billion this century, to a global population of at least ten and possibly twelve billion. As with food scarcity, much of the growth is expected in parts of the world already most strained by water shortage—in this case, urban Africa. In many African countries already, you are expected to get by on as little as twenty liters of water each day—less than half of what water organizations say is necessary for public health. As soon as 2030, global water demand is expected to outstrip supply by 40 percent.

Today, the crisis is political—which is to say, not beyond our capacity to fix. Water is an abundant resource made scarce through governmental neglect and indifference, bad infrastructure and contamination, careless urbanization and development. In other words, there is no need for a water crisis, but we have one anyway and aren't doing much to address it. Some cities lose more water to leaks than they deliver to homes: even in the United States, leaks and theft account for an estimated loss of 16 percent of fresh water; in Brazil, the estimate is 40 percent. In both cases, as everywhere, scarcity plays out so nakedly on a stage defined by have-and-have-not inequities that the resulting drama of resource competition can hardly be called, truly, a competition; the deck is so stacked that water shortage looks more like a tool of inequality. The global result is that as many as 2.1 billion people around the world do not have access to safe drinking water, and 4.5 billion don't have safely managed water for sanitation.

Like global warming, the water crisis is soluble—at present. But that 0.007 percent leaves an awfully thin margin, and climate change will cut into it. Half of the world's population depends on seasonal melt from high-elevation snow and ice, deposits that are dramatically threatened by warming. Even if we hit the Paris targets, the glaciers of the Himalayas will lose 40 percent of their ice, or possibly more, by 2100, and there could be widespread water shortages in Peru and California as the result of glacier melt. At four degrees warmer, the snow-capped Alps could look more like Morocco's Atlas Mountains, with 70 percent less snow by the end of this century. Overall, according to the United Nations, five billion people could have poor access to fresh water by 2050.

The United States won't be spared—boomtown Phoenix is, for instance, already in emergency planning mode, which should not surprise, given that even London is beginning to worry over water shortages. But given the reassurances of wealth—which can buy stopgap solutions and additional short-term supply—the United States will not be the worst hit. In India already, 600 million people face "high to extreme water stress," according to a 2018 government report, and 200,000 people die each year from lacking water or from contaminated water. By 2030, according to the same report, India will have only half the water it needs. In 1947, when the country was formed, per capita water availability in Pakistan stood at 5,000 cubic meters; today, thanks mostly to population growth, it is at 1,000; and soon, continued growth and climate change will bring it down to 400.

In the last hundred years, many of the planet's largest lakes have begun drying up, from the Aral Sea in Central Asia, which was once the world's fourth-largest and which has lost more than 90 percent of its volume in recent decades, to Lake Mead, which supplies much of Las Vegas's water and has lost as much as 400 billion gallons in a single year. Lake Poopó, once Bolivia's second-biggest, has completely disappeared; Iran's Lake Urmia has shrunk more than 80 percent in thirty years. Lake Chad, in Africa, has more or less evaporated entirely. Climate change is only one factor in this story, but its impact is not going to shrink over time.

As a short-term fix for the world's drought boom, we're already racing to drain underground water deposits, known as aquifers, but those deposits took millions of years to accumulate and aren't coming back anytime soon. In the United States, aquifers already supply a fifth of our water needs; as Brian Clark Howard has noted, wells that used to draw water at 500 feet now require pumps at least twice as deep. The Colorado River Basin, which serves water to seven states, lost twelve cubic miles of groundwater between 2004 and 2013; the Ogallala Aquifer in part of the Texas Panhandle lost 15 feet in a decade and is expected to drain by 70 percent in Kansas over the next fifty years.

We frequently choose to obsess over personal consumption, in part because it is within our control and in part as a contemporary form of virtue signaling. But ultimately those choices are, in almost all cases, trivial contributors, ones that blind us to the more important forces. When it comes to fresh water, the bigger picture is this: personal consumption amounts to such a thin sliver that only in the most extreme droughts can it even make a difference. In California, where droughts are punctuated by outrage over pools and ever-green lawns, total urban consumption accounts for only 10 percent.

And while agriculture is often hit the hardest by shortages, water issues are not exclusively rural. Fourteen of the world's twenty biggest cities are currently experiencing water scarcity or drought. Four billion people, it is estimated, already live in regions facing water shortages at least one month each year—that's about two-thirds of the planet's population. Half a billion are in places where the shortages never end. Today, at just one degree of warming, those regions with at least a month of water shortages each year include just about all of the United States west of Texas, where lakes and aquifers are being drained to meet demand, and stretch up into western Canada and down to Mexico City; almost all of North Africa and the Middle East; a large chunk of India; almost all of Australia; significant parts of Argentina and Chile; and everything in Africa south of Zambia.

As long as it has had advocates, climate change has been sold under a saltwater banner—melting Arctic, rising seas, shrinking coastlines. A freshwater crisis is more alarming, since we depend on fresh water far more acutely. It is also closer at hand. But while the planet commands the necessary resources today to provide water for drinking and sanitation to all the world's people, there is not the necessary political will—or even the inclination—to do so.

Over the next three decades, water demand from the global food system is expected to increase by about 50 percent, from cities and industry by 50 to 70 percent, and from energy by 85 percent. And climate change, with its coming megadroughts, promises to tighten supply considerably. In fact, the World Bank, in its landmark study of water and climate change "High and Dry," found that "the impacts of climate change will be channeled primarily through the water cycle." The bank's foreboding warning: when it comes to the cruelly cascading effects of climate change, water efficiency is as pressing a problem, and as important a puzzle to solve, as energy efficiency.

Peter Gleick of the Pacific Institute lists nearly five hundred water-related conflicts since 1900; almost half of the entire list is since 2010. Part of that, Gleick acknowledges, is a reflection of the relative abundance of recent data, and part of it is the changing nature of war—conflicts that used to unfold almost exclusively between states are now likely to spark within states and between groups. The five-year Syrian drought that stretched from 2006 to 2011, producing crop failures that created political instability and helped usher in the civil war that produced a global refugee crisis, is one vivid example.

"There's a saying in the water community," Gleick tells me. "If climate change is a shark, the water resources are the teeth."

Dying Oceans

WE TEND TO SEE OCEANS AS UNFATHOMABLE, THE CLOSEST thing we have on this planet to outer space: dark, forbidding, and, especially in the depths, quite weird and mysterious. "Who has known the ocean?" Rachel Carson wrote in her essay "Undersea," published twenty-five years before she tackled the desecration of the planet's land by human hands and industrial "cure-alls" in *Silent Spring*: "Neither you nor I, with our earth-bound senses, know the foam and surge of the tide that beats over the crab hiding under the seaweed of his tide-pool home; or the lilt of the long, slow swells of mid-ocean, where shoals of wandering fish prey and are preyed upon, and the dolphin breaks the waves to breathe the upper atmosphere."

But the ocean isn't the other. We are. Water is not a beachside attraction for land animals: at 70 percent of the earth's surface it is, by an enormous margin, the planet's predominant environment. Along with everything else it does, oceans feed us: globally, seafood accounts for nearly a fifth of all animal protein in the human diet, and in coastal areas, it can provide much more. The oceans also maintain our planetary seasons, through prehistoric currents like the Gulf Stream, and modulate the temperature of the planet, absorbing much of the heat of the sun.

Perhaps "has fed," "has maintained," and "has modulated" are better terms, since global warming threatens to undermine each one of those functions. Already, fish populations have migrated north by hundreds of miles in search of colder waters—flounder by 250 miles off the American East Coast, mackerel so far from their Continental home that the fishermen chasing them are no longer bound by rules set by the European Union. One study tracing human impact on marine life found only 13 percent of the ocean undamaged, and parts of the Arctic have been so transformed by warming that scientists are beginning to wonder how long they can keep calling those waters "arctic." And however much sea-level rise and coastal flooding have dominated our fears about the impact of climate change on the planet's ocean water, there is much more than just that to worry over.

At present, more than a fourth of the carbon emitted by humans is sucked up by the oceans, which also, in the past fifty years, have absorbed 90 percent of global warming's excess heat. Half of that heat has been absorbed since 1997, and the seas in 2020 carried at least 15 percent more heat energy than they did in the year 2000—absorbing three times as much additional energy, in just those two decades, as is contained in the entire planet's fossil fuel reserves. The result of all that carbon dioxide absorption is called "ocean acidification," which is exactly what it sounds like and which is also already burning through some of the planet's water basins. All on its own—through its effect on phytoplankton, which release sulfur into the air that helps cloud formation—ocean acidification could add between a quarter and a half of a degree of warming.

You have probably heard of "coral bleaching"—that is, coral dying—in which warmer ocean waters strip reefs of the protozoa, called zooxanthellae, that provide, through photosynthesis, up to 90 percent of the energy needs of the coral. Each reef is an ecosystem as complex as a modern city, and the zooxanthellae are its food supply, the basic building block of an energy chain; when they die, the whole complex is starved with military efficiency, like a city under siege or blockade. Since 2016, as much as half of Australia's landmark Great Barrier Reef has been stripped in this way. These large-scale die-outs are called "mass bleaching events"; one unfolded, globally, from 2014 to 2017. According to the World Resources Institute, by just 2030, ocean warming and acidification will threaten 90 percent of all reefs. According to the IPCC, two degrees of warming will likely kill all of them.

This is very bad news, because reefs support as much as a

quarter of all marine life and supply food and income for half a billion people. They also protect against flooding from storm surges—a function that offers value in the many billions, with reefs presently worth at least $400 million annually to Indonesia, the Philippines, Malaysia, Cuba, and Mexico—that is, $400 million annually to each. Ocean acidification will also damage fish populations directly. Though scientists aren't yet sure how to predict the effects on the stuff we haul out of the ocean to eat, they do know that in acid waters, oysters and mussels will struggle to grow their shells, and that rising carbon concentrations will impair fishes' sense of smell—which you may not have known they have but which often aids in their navigation. Off the coasts of Australia, fish populations have declined an estimated 32 percent in just ten years.

It has become quite common to say that we are living through a mass extinction—a period in which human activity has multiplied the rate at which species are disappearing from the earth by a factor perhaps as large as a thousand. It is probably also fair to call this an era marked by "ocean anoxification." The amount of ocean water with no oxygen at all has quadrupled globally over the past fifty years, giving us a total of more than four hundred "dead zones"; oxygen-deprived zones have grown by several million square kilometers, roughly the size of all of Europe; and hundreds of coastal cities now sit on fetid, under-oxygenated ocean. This is partly due to the simple warming of the planet, since warmer waters can carry less oxygen. But it is also partly the result of straightforward pollution—a recent Gulf of Mexico dead zone, all 9,000 square miles of it, was powered by the runoff of fertilizer chemicals washing into the Mississippi River from the industrial farms of the Midwest. In 2014, a not-atypical toxic event struck Lake Erie when fertilizer from corn and soy farms in Ohio spawned an algae bloom that cut off drinking water for Toledo. And in 2018, a dead zone the size of Florida was discovered in the Arabian Sea—so big that researchers believed it might encompass the entire 63,700-square-mile Gulf of Oman, or seven times the size of the dead zone in the Gulf of Mexico. "The ocean," said the lead researcher Bastien Queste, "is suffocating."

And then there is the possible slowdown of the "ocean conveyor belt," the great circulatory system made up of the Gulf Stream and other currents that is the primary way the planet regulates regional temperatures. How does this work? The water of the Gulf Stream cools off in the atmosphere of the Norwegian Sea, making the water itself denser, which sends it down into the bottom of the ocean, where it is then pushed southward by more Gulf Stream water—itself having cooled in the north and fallen to the ocean floor—eventually all the way to Antarctica, where the cold water returns to the surface and begins to heat up and travel north. The trip can take a thousand years.

As soon as the conveyor belt became the subject of real study, in the 1980s, there were oceanographers who worried it might shut down, which would lead to a dramatic disequilibration, or imbalance, of the planet's climate—the hotter parts getting much hotter and the colder parts much colder.

Today, a shutdown of the conveyor belt is not a scenario that any credible scientists worry about on any human timescale. But a slowdown is another matter. Already, climate change has depressed the velocity of the Gulf Stream by as much as 15 percent, a development that scientists call "an unprecedented event in the past millennium," believed to be one reason the sea-level rise along the East Coast of the United States is dramatically higher than elsewhere in the world. And in 2018, two major papers triggered a new wave of concern over the conveyor belt, technically called Atlantic Meridional Overturning Circulation, which was found to be moving at its slowest rate in at least 1,500 years. This happened about a hundred years ahead of the schedule of even alarmed scientists, and it marked what the climate scientist Michael E. Mann called, ominously, a tipping point. Further change, of course, is to come: the transformation of the ocean by warming make these unknown waters doubly unknowable, remodeling the planet's seas before we ever were able to discover their depths and all the life submerged there.

Unbreathable Air

OUR LUNGS NEED OXYGEN, BUT IT IS ONLY A FRACTION OF what we breathe, and the fraction tends to decline the more carbon is in the atmosphere. That doesn't mean we are at risk of suffocation—oxygen is far too abundant for that—but we will nevertheless suffer. With CO_2 at 930 parts per million (more than double where we are today), cognitive ability declines by 21 percent.

The effects are more pronounced indoors, where CO_2 tends to build up—that's one reason you probably feel a little more awake when taking a brisk walk outside than you do after spending a long day inside with the windows closed. And it's also a reason elementary school classrooms have been found by one study to already average 1,000 parts per million, with almost a quarter of those surveyed in Texas over 3,000—quite alarming numbers, given that these are the environments we've designed to promote intellectual performance. But classrooms are not the worst offenders: other studies have shown even higher concentrations on airplanes, with effects that you can probably groggily recall from past experience.

But carbon is, more or less, the least of it. Going forward, the planet's air won't just be warmer; it will likely also be dirtier, more oppressive, and more sickening. Droughts have a direct impact on air quality, producing what is now known as dust exposure and in the days of the American Dust Bowl was called "dust pneumonia"; climate change will bring new dust storms to those plains states, where deaths from dust pollution are expected to more than double and hospitalizations to triple. The hotter the planet gets, the more ozone forms, and by the middle of this century, Americans should suffer a 70 percent increase in days with unhealthy ozone smog, the National Center for Atmospheric Research has projected. By the 2090s, depending on what pollution path we take, as many as two billion people globally could be breathing air above the WHO (World Health Organization) "safe" level. Already, more than 10,000 people die from air pollution every day. Annually, the figure is ten million per year.

Pollution like this isn't news in any meaningful sense; you can find omens about the toxicity of smog and the dangers of blackened air, for instance, in the writing of Charles Dickens, rarely appreciated as an environmentalist. But every year, we are discovering more and more ways in which our industrial activity is poisoning the planet.

One particular note of alarm has been struck by what seems like an entirely new—or newly understood—pollution threat: microplastics. Global warming did not bring us microplastics in any direct way; the world's booming consumer culture is to blame.

Environmentalists probably know already about "the Great Pacific garbage patch"—that mass of plastic, twice the size of Texas, floating freely in the Pacific Ocean. It is not actually an island—in fact, it is not actually a stable mass, only rhetorically convenient for us to think of it that way. And it is mostly composed of larger-scale plastics, of the kind visible to the human eye. The microscopic bits—700,000 of them can be released into the surrounding environment by a single washing-machine cycle—are more insidious. And, believe it or not, more pervasive: a quarter of fish sold in Indonesia and California contain plastics, according to one recent study. European eaters of shellfish, one estimate has suggested, consume at least 11,000 bits each year.

The direct effect on ocean life is even more striking. The total number of marine species said to be adversely affected by plastic pollution has risen from 260 in 1995, when the first assessment was carried out, to 690 in 2015 and 1,450 in 2018. A majority of fish tested in the Great Lakes contained microplastics, as did the guts of 73 percent of fish surveyed in the northwest Atlantic. One UK supermarket study found that every 100 grams of mussels were infested with 70 particles of plastic. Some fish have learned to eat plastic, and certain species of krill are now functioning as plastic processing plants, churning microplastics into smaller bits, which scientists are now calling "nanoplastics." But krill can't grind it all down; in one square mile of water near Toronto, 3.4 million microplastic particles were recently trawled. Of course, seabirds are not immune: one researcher found 225 pieces of plastic in the stomach of a single three-month-old chick, weighing 10 percent of its body mass—the equivalent of an average human carrying about ten to twenty pounds of plastic in a distended belly. ("Imagine having to take your first flight out to sea with all that in your stomach," the researcher told the *Financial Times,* adding, "Around the world, seabirds are declining faster than any other bird group.")

Microplastics have been found in beer, honey, and sixteen of seventeen tested brands of commercial sea salt, across eight different countries. The more we test, the more we find; microplastics have been found in Arctic snow and the breast milk of new mothers. We can breathe in microplastics, even when indoors, where they've been detected suspended in the air, and do already drink them: they are found in the tap water of 94 percent of all tested American cities. And global plastic production is expected to triple by 2050, when there will be more plastic in the ocean than fish.

Plagues of Warming

ROCK IS A RECORD OF PLANETARY HISTORY, ERAS AS LONG AS millions of years flattened by the forces of geological time into strata with amplitudes of just inches, or just an inch, or even less. Ice works that way, too, as a climate ledger, but it is also frozen history, some of which can be reanimated when unfrozen. There are now, trapped in Arctic ice, diseases that have not circulated in the air for millions of years—in some cases, since before humans were around to encounter them. Which means our immune systems would have no idea how to fight back when those prehistoric plagues emerge from the ice. Already, in laboratories, several microbes have been reanimated: a 32,000-year-old "extremophile" bacteria revived in 2005, an 8-million-year-old bug brought back to life in 2007, a 3.5-million-year-old one a Russian scientist self-injected, out of curiosity, just to see what would happen. (He survived.) In 2018, scientists revived something a bit bigger—a worm that had been frozen in permafrost for the last 42,000 years.

These frozen organisms aren't very likely to survive the thaw; those that have been brought back to life have been reanimated typically under fastidious lab conditions. But in 2016, a boy was killed and twenty others infected by anthrax that was released when retreating permafrost exposed the frozen carcass of a reindeer killed by the bacteria at least seventy-five years earlier; more than two thousand present-day reindeer died.

What concerns epidemiologists more than ancient diseases are existing scourges relocated, rewired, or even re-evolved by warming. The first effect is geographical. Before the early modern period, human provinciality was a guard against pandemic—a bug could wipe out a town or a kingdom, or even in an extreme case devastate a continent—but in most instances, it couldn't travel much farther than its victims, which is to say, not very far at all. The Black Death killed as much as 60 percent of Europe in the fourteenth century, but consider, for a gruesome counterfactual, how big its impact might have been in a truly globalized world.

Today, even with globalization and the rapid intermingling of human populations, our ecosystems are mostly stable, and this functions as another limit—we know where certain bugs can spread and know the environments in which they cannot. (This is why certain vectors of adventure tourism require dozens of new vaccines and prophylactic medications, and why New Yorkers traveling to London don't need to worry.)

But global warming will scramble those ecosystems, meaning it will help disease trespass those limits as surely as Cortés did in the fifteenth century. That is why some researchers have described the coming age as a "Pandemicine." The footprint of every mosquito-borne illness is presently circumscribed, but those borders are disappearing rapidly, as the tropics expand—the current rate is thirty miles per decade. In Brazil, for generations, yellow fever sat in the Amazon basin, where the *Haemagogus* and *Sabethes* mosquitoes thrived, making the disease a concern for those who lived, worked, or traveled deep into the jungle, but only for them; in 2016, it left the Amazon, as more and more mosquitoes fanned out of the rain forest; and by 2017, it had reached areas around the country's megalopolises, São Paulo and Rio de Janeiro—more than thirty million people, many of them living in shantytowns, facing the arrival of a disease that kills between 3 and 8 percent of those infected.

Yellow fever is just one of the plagues that will be carried by mosquitoes as they migrate, conquering more and more of a warming world—the globalization of pandemic disease. Malaria alone kills a million people each year already, infecting many more, but you don't worry much about it if you are living in Maine or France. As the tropics creep northward and mosquitoes migrate with them, you may; over the course of the next century, more and more of the world's population will be living under the shadow of diseases like these. Unless, that is, the world endeavors to purposefully drive them to extinction, as some researchers are considering already.

Projections like those depend not just on climate models but on an intricate understanding of the organism at play. Or, rather, organisms. Malaria transmission involves both the disease and the mosquito; Lyme disease, both the disease and the tick—which is another epidemiologically threatening creature whose universe is rapidly expanding, thanks to global warming. As Mary Beth Pfeiffer has documented, Lyme case counts have spiked in Japan, Turkey, and South Korea, where the disease was literally nonexistent as recently as 2010—zero cases—and now lives inside hundreds more Koreans each year. In the Netherlands, 54 percent of the country's land is now infested; in Europe as a whole, Lyme caseloads are now three times the standard level. In the United States, there are likely around 300,000 new infections each year—and since many of those treated for Lyme continue to show symptoms years after treatment, the numbers can stockpile. Overall, the number of disease cases from mosquitoes, ticks, and fleas have tripled in the United States over just the last thirteen years, with dozens of counties across the country encountering ticks for the first time. But the effects of the epidemic can be seen perhaps most clearly in animals other than humans: in

Minnesota during the 2000s, winter ticks helped drop the moose population by 58 percent in a single decade. In New England, dead moose calves have been found suckling as many as 90,000 engorged ticks, often killing the calves not through Lyme disease but simple anemia, the effect of that number of bugs each drawing a few milliliters of blood from the moose. Those that survive are far from robust, many having scratched so incessantly at their own hides to clear it of ticks that they completely eliminated their hair, leaving behind a spooky gray skin that has earned them the name "ghost moose."

Lyme is still, in relative terms, a young disease, and one we don't yet understand all that well: we attribute a very mysterious and incoherent set of symptoms to it, from joint pain to fatigue to memory loss to facial palsy, almost as a catchall explanation for ailments we cannot pinpoint in patients who we know have been bitten by a bug carrying the bug. We do know ticks, however, as surely as we know malaria—there are not many parasites we understand better. But there are many, many millions we understand worse, which means our sense of how climate change will redirect or remodel them is shrouded in a foreboding ignorance. And then there are the plagues that climate change will confront us with for the very first time—a whole new universe of diseases humans have never before even known to worry about.

"New universe" is not hyperbole. Scientists guess the planet could harbor more than a million yet-to-be-discovered viruses. Bacteria are even trickier, and so we probably know about even fewer of them.

Perhaps scariest are those that live within us, peacefully for now. More than 99 percent of bacteria inside human bodies are presently unknown to science, which means we are operating in near-total ignorance about the effects climate change might have on the bugs in, for instance, our guts—about how many of the bacteria modern humans have come to rely on, like unseen factory workers, for everything from digesting our food to modulating our anxiety, could be rewired, diminished, or entirely killed off by an additional few degrees of heat.

Overwhelmingly, of course, the viruses and bacteria making homes inside us are nonthreatening to humans at present. Presumably, a difference of a degree or two in global temperature won't dramatically change the behavior of the majority of them— probably the vast majority, even the overwhelming majority. But consider the case of the saiga—the adorable, dwarflike antelope native to Central Asia. In May 2015, nearly two-thirds of the global population died in the span of just days—every single saiga in an area the size of Florida, the land suddenly dotted with hundreds of thousands of saiga carcasses and not one lone survivor. An event like this is called a mega-death, this one so striking and cinematic that it immediately gave rise to a whole raft of conspiracy theories: aliens, radiation, dumped rocket fuel. But no toxins were found by researchers poking through the killing fields—in the animals themselves, in the soil, in the local plants. The culprit, it turned out, was a simple bacterium, *Pasteurella multocida,* which had lived inside the saiga's tonsils, without threatening its host in any way, for many, many generations. Suddenly it had proliferated, emigrated to the bloodstream, and from there to the animals' liver, kidneys, and spleen. Why? "The places where the saigas died in May 2015 were extremely warm and humid," Ed Yong wrote in *The Atlantic*. "In fact, humidity levels were the highest ever seen in the region since records began in 1948. The same pattern held for two earlier, and much smaller, die-offs from 1981 and 1988. When the temperature gets really hot, and the air gets really wet, saiga die. Climate is the trigger, *Pasteurella* is the bullet."

Economic Collapse

YOU DO NOT HAVE TO BELIEVE THAT ECONOMIC GROWTH IS A mirage produced by fossil fumes to worry that climate change is a threat to it—in fact, this proposition forms the cornerstone on which an entire edifice of academic literature has been built during the last decade. The vanguard research about the economics of warming has come from Solomon Hsiang and Marshall Burke and Edward Miguel, who are not historians of fossil capitalism but who offer some very bleak analysis of their own: in a country that's already relatively warm, every degree Celsius of warming reduces growth, on average, by about one percentage point (an enormous number, considering we count growth in the low single digits as "strong"). Compared to the trajectory of economic growth with no climate change, their average projection in a high-end emissions scenario is for a 23 percent loss in per capita earning globally by the end of this century.

The breakdown by country is perhaps even more alarming. Even given worst-case warming, there are places that benefit, in the north, where warmer temperatures can improve agriculture and economic productivity: Canada, Russia, Scandinavia, Greenland. But in the midlatitudes, the countries that produce the bulk of the world's economic activity—the United States, China—would lose nearly half of their potential output. The warming near the equator would be worse, with losses from Mexico to Brazil, throughout Africa, and in India and Southeast Asia approaching 100 percent. India alone, one study proposed, would shoulder nearly a quarter of the economic suffering inflicted on the entire world by climate change. In 2018, the World Bank estimated that the current path of carbon emissions would sharply diminish the living conditions of 800 million living throughout South Asia. One hundred million, they say, will be dragged into extreme poverty by climate change just over the next decade. Perhaps "back into" is more appropriate: many of the most vulnerable populations are those that have just extracted themselves from deprivation and subsistence living, through developing-world growth powered by industrialization and fossil fuel.

We've gotten used to setbacks on our erratic march along the arc of economic history, but we know them as setbacks and expect elastic recoveries. What climate change has in store is not that kind of thing—not a Great Recession or a Great Depression but, in economic terms, a permanent dampening.

How could that come to be? The answer is partly in the preceding chapters—natural disaster, flooding, public health crises. All of these are not just tragedies but expensive tragedies, and they are beginning already to accumulate at an unprecedented rate. There is the cost to agriculture, and to real estate.

But there is a direct cost of heat to growth, as there is to health. Some of these effects we can see already—for instance, warped train tracks or the grounding of flights due to temperatures so high that they abolish the aerodynamics that allow planes to take off, which is now commonplace at heat-stricken airports like the one in Phoenix. (But keep in mind that every round-trip plane ticket from New York to London costs the Arctic thirty-two more square feet of ice.) From Switzerland to Finland, heat waves have necessitated closing power plants when cooling liquids have become too hot to do their job. And in India, in 2012, 670 million lost power when the country's grid was overwhelmed by farmers irrigating their fields without the help of the monsoon season, which never arrived. In all but the shiniest projects in all but the wealthiest parts of the world, the planet's infrastructure was simply not built for climate change, which means the vulnerabilities are everywhere you look.

Other, less obvious effects are also visible—for instance, productivity. For the past few decades, economists have wondered why the computer revolution and the internet have not brought meaningful productivity gains to the industrialized world. Spreadsheets, database management software, email—these innovations alone would seem to promise huge gains in efficiency for any business or economy adopting them. But those gains simply haven't materialized; in fact, the economic period in which those innovations were introduced, along with literally thousands of similar computer-driven efficiencies, has been characterized, especially in the developed West, by wage and productivity stagnation and dampened economic growth. One speculative possibility: computers have made us more efficient and productive, but at the same time climate change has had the opposite effect, diminishing or entirely wiping out the impact of technology. How could this be? One theory is the negative cognitive effects of direct heat and air pollution, both of which are accumulating more research support by the day. And whether or not that theory explains the great stagnation of the last several decades, we do know that, globally, warmer temperatures do dampen worker productivity.

Overall, though it will be hit hard by climate impacts, the United States is among the most well positioned to endure—its wealth and geography are reasons that America has only begun to register the effects of climate change that already plague warmer and poorer parts of the world. But in part because it has so much to lose, and in part because it so aggressively developed its very long coastlines, the US is more vulnerable to climate impacts than any country in the world but India, and its economic illness won't be quarantined at the border. In a globalized world, there is what Zhengtao Zhang and others call an "economic ripple effect." They've also quantified this effect and found that the impact grows along with warming. At one degree Celsius, with a decline in American GDP of 0.88 percent, global GDP would fall by 0.12 percent, with the American losses cascading through the world system. At two degrees, the economic ripple effect triples, though here, too, the effects play out differently in different parts of the world; compared to the impact of American losses at one degree, at two degrees the economic ripple effect in China would be 4.5 times larger. The radiating shock waves issuing from other countries are smaller because their economies are smaller, but the waves will be coming from nearly every country in the world, like radio signals beamed out from a whole global forest of towers, each transmitting economic suffering.

For better or for worse, in the countries of the wealthy West, we have settled on economic growth as the single best metric, however imperfect, of the health of our societies. Of course, using that metric, climate change registers—with its wildfires and droughts and famines, it registers seismically. The costs are astronomical already, with single hurricanes now delivering damage in the hundreds of billions of dollars. Should the planet warm 3.7 degrees, one assessment suggests, climate change damages could total $551 trillion—nearly twice as much wealth as exists in the world today. We are on track for more warming still.

Climate Conflict

"BATTLE"—BEFORE RUSSIA'S INVASION OF UKRAINE, "BATTLE"—
the word might have felt like a relic. In the wealthy West, we had
come to pretend that war is an anomalous feature of modern life,
since it seemed to have been retired as fully from our everyday experience as polio. But globally, there are nineteen ongoing armed
conflicts hot enough to claim at least a thousand lives each year.

That all of these counts are expected to spike in the coming
decades is one reason that, as nearly every climate scientist I've
spoken to has pointed out, the US military is obsessed with climate change. The Pentagon issues regular climate threat assessments and make plans for a new era of conflict governed by global
warming. The drowning of American navy bases by sea-level rise
is trouble enough, and the melting of the Arctic promises to open
an entirely new theater of conflict, once nearly as foreign-seeming
as the space race.

But for the military, climate change is not just a matter of great-power rivalry executed across a transformed map. Even for those in the American military who expect the country's hegemony to endure indefinitely, climate change presents a problem, because being the world's policeman is quite a bit harder when the crime rate doubles. And it's not just Syria where climate has contributed to civil war. Some speculate that the elevated level of strife across the Middle East over the past generation reflects the pressures of global warming—a hypothesis all the more cruel considering that warming began to accelerate when the industrialized world extracted and burned the region's oil. From Boko Haram to ISIS to the Taliban and militant Islamic groups in Pakistan, drought and crop failure have been linked to radicalization, and the effect may be especially pronounced amid ethnic strife: a 2016 study found that, from 1980 to 2010, 23 percent of conflict in the world's ethnically diverse countries began in months stamped by weather disaster. According to one assessment, thirty-two countries—from Haiti to the Philippines and India to Cambodia, each heavily dependent on farming and agriculture—face "extreme risk" of conflict and civil unrest from climate disruptions over the next thirty years.

What accounts for the relationship between climate and conflict? Some of it comes down to agriculture and economics: when crop yields drop and productivity falls, societies can falter, and when droughts and heat waves hit, the shocks can be felt even more deeply, electrifying political fault lines and producing or exposing other dangers no one knew to worry over. A lot has to do with the forced migration that can result from those shocks and with the political and social instability that migration often produces; when things go south, those who are able tend to flee, not always to places ready to welcome them—in fact, recent history shows, often quite the opposite. And today migration is already at a record high, with displaced people numbering in the tens of millions wandering the planet right now. That is the outbound impact; but the local one is often more profound. Those who remain in a region ravaged by extreme weather can find themselves navigating an entirely new social and political structure, if one endures at all. And it is not just weak states that can fall at the hands of climate pressures; in recent years, scholars have compiled a long list of empires buckled, at least in part, by climate effects and events: Egyptian, Akkaddian, Roman.

This complex calculus is what makes researchers reluctant to assign blame for conflict neatly, but complexity is how warming articulates its brutality. Like the cost to growth, war is not a discrete impact of global temperature rise but something more like an all-encompassing aggregation of climate change's worst tremors and cascades. Climate is, thus, not the sole cause but the spark igniting a complex bundle of social kindling. Most wars throughout history, it is important to remember, have been conflicts over resources, often ignited by resource scarcity, which is what an earth densely populated and denuded by climate change will yield. Those wars don't tend to increase resources; most of the time, they incinerate them.

"Systems"

WHAT I CALL CASCADES, CLIMATE SCIENTISTS CALL "SYSTEMS crises." These crises are what the American military means when it refers to climate change as a "threat multiplier." The multiplication, when it falls short of conflict, produces migration—that is, climate refugees. Since 2008, by one count, it has already produced 22 million of them.

In the West, some people think of refugees as a problem that the broken and impoverished parts of the world inflict on relatively more stable, and wealthier, societies. But Hurricane Harvey produced at least 60,000 climate migrants in Texas, and Hurricane Irma forced the evacuation of nearly 7 million. As with so much else, it will only get worse from here. By 2100, sea-level rise alone could displace 13 million Americans—a few percent of the country's total population. If emissions decline, or if the planet's

ice melts more slowly than scientists fear, the numbers this century would be smaller, but in the long term the picture would
remain the same. Many of those sea-level refugees will come
from the country's southeast—chiefly Florida, where 2.5 million
are expected to be flooded out of greater Miami, and Louisiana,
where the New Orleans area is predicted to lose half a million.

As an unusually wealthy country, the United States is, for now,
unusually suited to withstand such disruptions—one can almost
imagine, over the course of a century, tens of millions of resettled
Americans adapting to a ravaged coastline and a new geography for the country. Almost. But warming is not just a matter
of sea level, and its horrors will not hit nations like the United
States first. In fact, the impacts will be greatest in the world's
least developed, most impoverished, and therefore least resilient
nations—almost literally a story of the world's rich drowning the
world's poor with their waste. The first country to industrialize
and produce greenhouse gas on a grand scale, the United Kingdom, is expected to suffer least from climate change. The world's
slowest-developing countries, producing the least emissions, will
be among those hardest hit; the climate system of the Democratic
Republic of the Congo, one of the world's poorest countries, is
scheduled to be especially profoundly perturbed.

Congo is mostly landlocked and mountainous, but in the next
generation of warming, those features will not be protections.
Wealth will be a buffer for some countries, but not a safeguard, as
Australia is learning already: by far the richest of all the countries

staring down the most intense, most immediate warming barrages, it is an early test case of how the world's affluent societies will bend, or buckle, or rebuild under the pressure of temperature changes likely to hit the rest of the well-off world only later this century. In 2011, a single heat wave there produced significant tree dieback and coral bleaching, the death of plant life, crashes in local bird populations and dramatic spikes in the number of certain insects, and transformations of ecosystems both marine and terrestrial. When the country enacted a carbon tax, its emissions fell; when, under political pressure, the tax was repealed, they rose again. In 2018, the country's parliament declared global warming a "current and existential national security risk." A few months later, its climate-conscious prime minister was forced to resign, for the shame of attempting to honor the Paris Accords.

More than 140 million people in just three regions of the world will be made climate migrants by 2050, the World Bank projected in a 2018 study, assuming current warming and emissions trends—86 million in sub-Saharan Africa, 40 million in South Asia, and 17 million in Latin America. The most commonly cited estimate from the United Nations' International Organization for Migration (IOM) suggests numbers a bit higher—200 million total by 2050. Some figures even run higher. According to the UN's IOM, climate change may create as many as a billion migrants in the world by 2050. That figure is quite high, higher than most non-advocates credit. But one billion is about as many people as live today in North and South America combined. Imagine the two continents suddenly drowned in the sea, the whole New World submerged, and everyone left bobbing at the surface, fighting for a foothold somewhere, anywhere, and, if someone else is scrambling for the same dry spot, scrambling to get there first.

The system in crisis is not always "society"; the system can also be the body. Historically, in the United States, more than two-thirds of outbreaks of waterborne disease—illnesses smuggled into humans through algae and bacteria that can produce gastro-intestinal problems—were preceded by unusually intense rainfall, disrupting local water supplies. The concentration of salmonella in streams, for instance, increases significantly after heavy rainfall, and the country's most dramatic outbreak of waterborne disease came in 1993, when more than 400,000 in Milwaukee fell ill from cryptosporidium immediately after a storm.

Sudden rainfall shocks—both deluges and their opposite, droughts—can devastate agricultural communities economically but also produce what scientists call, with understatement, "nutritional deficiencies" in fetuses and infants In Vietnam, those who passed through that crucible early on, and survived, were shown to start school later in life, do worse when they got there, and grow less tall than their peers. In India, the same cycle-of-poverty pattern holds. The lifelong impacts of chronic malnutrition are more troubling still for being permanent: diminishing cognitive ability, flattened adult wages, increased morbidity. In Ecuador, climate damage has been seen even in middle-class children, who bear the mark of rainfall shocks and extreme temperatures on their wages twenty to sixty years after the fact. The effects begin in the womb, and they are universal, with measurable declines in lifetime earnings for every day over ninety degrees during a baby's nine months in utero. The impacts accumulate later in life, too. An enormous study in Taiwan found that, for every single unit of additional air pollution, the relative risk of Alzheimer's doubled. Similar patterns have been observed from Ontario to Mexico City.

As conditions of environmental degradation become more universal, it may, perversely, require more imagination to consider their costs. When the deprived are no longer outlier communities but instead are whole regions, whole countries, conditions that once may have seemed inhumane now appear, to a future generation who knows no better, simply "normal." In the past, we have looked in horror at the stunted growth of national populations who passed through famines both natural (Sudan, Somalia) and man-made (Yemen, North Korea). In the future, climate change may stunt us all, in one way or another, with no control group entirely spared.

In a world of suffering, the self-interested mind craves compartmentalization, and one of the most interesting frontiers of emerging climate science traces the imprint left on our psychological well-being by the force of global warming, which can overwhelm whatever methods we devise to cope—that is, the mental health effects of a world on fire. Perhaps the most predictable vector is trauma: between a quarter and a half of all those exposed to extreme weather events will experience them as an ongoing negative shock to their mental health. In England, flooding was found to quadruple levels of psychological distress, even among those in an inundated community but not personally affected by the flooding. In the aftermath of Hurricane Katrina, 62 percent of evacuees exceeded the diagnostic threshold for acute stress disorder; in the region as a whole, nearly a third had PTSD. Wildfires, curiously, yielded a lower incidence—just 24 percent of evacuees in the aftermath of one series of California blazes. But a third of those who lived through fire were diagnosed, in its aftermath, with depression.

Unsurprisingly, climate trauma is especially harsh in the young—in this, our folk wisdom about the impressionable minds of children is reliable. Thirty-two weeks after Hurricane Andrew hit Florida in 1992, killing forty, more than half of children surveyed had moderate PTSD and more than a third had a severe form; in the high-impact areas, 70 percent of children scored in the moderate-to-severe range fully twenty-one months after the Category 5 storm. By dismal contrast, soldiers returning from war are estimated to suffer from PTSD at a rate between 11 and 31 percent.

One especially detailed study examined the mental health

fallout from Hurricane Mitch, a Category 5 storm and the second-deadliest Atlantic hurricane on record, which struck Central America in 1998, leaving 11,000 dead. In Posoltega, the most-hard-hit region of Nicaragua, children had a 27 percent chance of having been seriously injured, a 31 percent chance of having lost a family member, and a 63 percent chance of their home having been damaged or destroyed. You can imagine the aftereffects. Ninety percent of adolescents in the area were left with PTSD, with the average adolescent boy registering at the high end of the range of severe PTSD, and the average teenage girl registering over the threshold of very severe. Six months after the storm, four out of every five teenage survivors from Posoltega suffered from depression; more than half, the study found, compulsively nursed what the authors called, a bit euphemistically, "vengeful thoughts."

And then there are the more surprising mental health costs. Climate affects both the onset and the severity of depression, *The Lancet* has reported. Rising temperature and humidity are married, in the data, to emergency-room visits for mental health issues. When it's hotter out, psychiatric hospitals see spikes in proper inpatient admissions as well. Schizophrenics, especially, are admitted at much higher rates when the temperatures are higher, and inside those hospitals, ward temperature significantly increases symptom severity in schizophrenic patients. Heat waves bring waves of other things, too: mood disorders, anxiety disorders, dementia.

Heat produces violence and conflict between people, we know, and so it should probably not surprise us that it also generates a spike in violence against oneself. Each increase of a single degree Celsius in monthly temperature is associated with almost a percentage point rise of the suicide rate in the United States, and more than two percentage points in Mexico; an unmitigated emissions scenario could produce 40,000 additional suicides in these countries by 2050. One startling paper by Tamma Carleton has suggested that global warming is already responsible for 59,000 suicides, many of them farmers, in India, where one-fifth of all the world's suicides now occur and where suicide rates have doubled since just 1980. When temperatures are already high, she found, a rise of just one additional degree, on a single day, will produce seventy additional corpses, each dead by the farmer's own hand.

If you have made it this far, you are a brave reader. Any one of these eleven chapters contains, by rights, enough horror to induce a panic attack in even the most optimistic of those considering climate change. But you are not merely considering it; you are about to embark on living it. In many cases, in many places, we already are.

In fact, what is perhaps most remarkable about all the research summarized to this point is that it is research emerging from the world we know today. That is, a world just one degree warmer; a world not yet deformed and defaced beyond recognition; a world bound largely by conventions devised in an age of climate stability, now barreling headlong into an age of something more like climate chaos, a world we are only beginning to perceive.

All of which means that the eleven threats described in these eleven chapters yield a portrait of the future only as best as it can be painted in the present. The map of our new world will be drawn in part by natural processes that remain mysterious, but more definitively by human hands. For the sake of clarity, I've treated each of the threats from climate change—sea-level rise, food scarcity, economic stagnation—as discrete threats, which they are not. Some may prove offsetting, some mutually reinforcing, and others merely adjacent. But together they form a latticework of climate crisis, beneath which at least some humans, and probably many billions, will live. How?

THE CLIMATE
KALEIDOSCOPE

Storytelling

ON-SCREEN, CLIMATE DEVASTATION IS EVERYWHERE YOU look, and yet nowhere in focus, as though we are displacing our anxieties about global warming by restaging them in theaters of our own design and control—perhaps out of hope that the end of days remains "fantasy." *Game of Thrones* opens with an unmistakable climate prophecy, but warns "winter is coming"; the premise of *Interstellar* is an environmental scourge, but the scourge is a crop blight. *Children of Men* depicts civilization in semi-collapse, but collapsed by a fertility menace. *Mad Max: Fury Road* unfurls like a global-warming panorama, a scrolling saga of a world made desert, but its political crisis comes, in fact, from an oil shortage. The protagonist of *The Last Man on Earth* is made that way by a sweeping virus, the family of *A Quiet Place* is hushed by giant insect predators lurking in the wilderness, and the central cataclysm of the "Apocalypse" season of *American Horror Story* is a throw-back—a nuclear winter. In the many zombie apocalypses of this era of ecological anxiety, the zombies are invariably rendered as an alien force, not an endemic one. That is, not as us.

What does it mean to be entertained by a fictional apocalypse as we stare down the possibility of a real one? One job of pop culture is always to serve stories that distract even as they appear to engage—to deliver sublimation and diversion. In a time of cascading climate change, Hollywood is also trying to make sense of our changing relationship to nature, which we have long regarded from at least an arm's length—but which, amid this change, has returned as a chaotic force we nevertheless understand, on some level, as our fault. The adjudication of that guilt is another thing entertainment can do, when law and public policy fail, though our culture, like our politics, specializes in assigning the blame to others—in projecting rather than accepting guilt. A form of emotional prophylaxis is also at work: in fictional stories of climate catastrophe, we may also be looking for catharsis and collectively trying to persuade ourselves we might survive it.

But the scope of the world's transformation may just as quickly eliminate the genre—indeed eliminate any effort to tell the story of warming, which could grow too large and too obvious even for Hollywood. You can tell stories "about" climate change while it still seems a marginal feature of human life, or an overwhelming feature of lives marginal to your own. But at three degrees of warming, or four, hardly anyone will be able to feel insulated from its impacts—or want to watch it on-screen as they watch it out their windows. And so as climate change expands across the horizon—as it begins to seem inescapable, total—it may cease to be a story and become, instead, an all-encompassing setting. Why watch or read science fiction about the world you can see plainly out your own window? At the moment, stories illustrating global warming can still offer an escapist pleasure, even if that pleasure often comes in the form of horror. But when we can no longer pretend that climate suffering is distant—in time or in place—we will stop pretending about it and start pretending within it.

In his book-length essay *The Great Derangement*, the Indian novelist Amitav Ghosh wonders why fiction hasn't yet made the dangers of warming sufficiently "real" to us, and why we haven't had a spate of novels in the genre he basically imagines into half existence and dubs "the environmental uncanny."

Others imagine "cli-fi," genre fiction that sounds environmental alarm, didactic adventure stories, often preachy in their politics. Ghosh has something else in mind: the great climate novel. "Consider, for example, the stories that congeal around questions like, 'Where were you when the Berlin Wall fell?' or 'Where were you on 9/11?'" he writes. "Will it ever be possible to ask, in the same vein, 'Where were you at 400 ppm?' or 'Where were you when the Larsen B ice shelf broke up?'"

His answer: probably not, because the dilemmas and dramas

of climate change are simply incompatible with the kinds of stories we tell ourselves about ourselves, especially in conventional novels, which tend to end with uplift and hope and to emphasize the journey of an individual conscience rather than the miasma of social fate. This is a narrow definition of the novel, but almost everything about our broader narrative culture suggests that climate change is a major mismatch of a subject for all the tools we have at hand. Ghosh's question applies even to comic-book movies that might theoretically illustrate global warming: Who would the heroes be? And what would they be doing? The puzzle probably helps explain why so many pop entertainments that do try to tackle climate change, from *The Day After Tomorrow* on, are so corny and pedantic: collective action is, dramatically, a snore.

The problem is even more acute in gaming, which is poised to join or even supplant novels and movies and television, and which is built, as a narrative genre, even more obsessively around the imperatives of the protagonist—i.e., you. It also promises at least a simulation of agency. That could grow more comforting in the coming years, assuming we continue to proceed, zombie-like ourselves, down a path to ruin. Already, the world's most popular game, *Fortnite*, invites players into a competition for scarce resources during an extreme weather event—as though you yourself might conquer and totally resolve the issue.

There is also, beyond the hero problem, a villain problem. Literary fiction may not accommodate epic stories of the kind for which climate change fashions a natural setting, but in the genre fiction and blockbuster movie space at least, we have a number of models at hand, from superhero sagas to alien-invasion narratives. Stories don't get more elemental and familiar than those that used to be described as "man against nature." But in *Moby-Dick* or *The Old Man and the Sea* or many lesser examples, nature was typically a metaphor, encasing a theological or metaphysical force. That was because nature remained mysterious, inexplicable. Climate change has changed that, too. We know the meaning of extreme weather and natural disaster, now, though they still arrive with a kind of prophetic majesty: the meaning is that there is more to come, and that it is our doing. You wouldn't have to do much in rewrites to *Independence Day* to reboot it as cli-fi. But, in the place of aliens, who would its heroes be fighting against? Ourselves?

Villainy was easier to grasp in stories depicting the prospect of nuclear Armageddon. The moral responsibility of climate change, however, is much murkier. Global warming isn't something that might happen should several people make some profoundly shortsighted calculations; it is something that is already happening, everywhere, and without anything like direct supervisors. Nuclear Armageddon, in theory, has a few dozen authors; climate catastrophe has billions of them, with responsibility distended over time and extended across much of the planet. This is not to say it is distributed evenly: though climate change will be given its ultimate dimensions by the course of industrialization in the developing world, at present the world's wealthy possess the lion's share of guilt—the richest 10 percent producing half of all emissions. This distribution tracks closely with global income inequality, which is one reason that many on the left point to the all-encompassing system, saying that industrial capitalism is to blame. It is. But saying so does not name an antagonist; it names a toxic investment vehicle with most of the world as stakeholders, many of whom eagerly bought in. And who, in fact, quite enjoy their present way of life. That includes, almost certainly, you and me and everyone else buying escapism with our Netflix subscription. Meanwhile, it simply isn't the case that the socialist countries of the world are behaving more responsibly, with carbon, nor that they have in the past.

Complicity does not make for good drama. Modern morality plays need antagonists, and the desire gets stronger when apportioning blame becomes a political necessity, which it surely will. This is a problem for stories both fictional and non-, each kind drawing logic and energy from the other. The natural villains are the oil companies—and in fact a recent survey of movies depicting climate apocalypse found the plurality were actually about corporate greed. But the impulse to assign them full responsibility is complicated by the fact that transportation and industry make up less than 40 percent of global emissions. The companies' disinformation-and-denial campaigns are probably a stronger case for villainy—a more grotesque performance of corporate evilness is hardly imaginable, and a generation from now, oil-backed denial will likely be seen as among the most heinous conspiracies against human health and well-being that have been perpetrated in the modern world. But evilness is not the same as responsibility, and climate denialism has captured just one political party in one country in the world—a country with only two of the world's ten biggest oil companies. American inaction surely slowed global progress on climate in a time when the world had only one superpower. But there is simply nothing like climate denialism beyond the US border, which encloses the production of only 15 percent of the world's emissions. To believe the fault for global warming lies exclusively with the Republican Party or its fossil fuel backers is a form of American narcissism.

That narcissism, I suspect, will be broken by climate change. In the rest of the world, where action on carbon is just as slow, and resistance to real policy changes just as strong, denial is simply not a problem. The corporate influence of fossil fuel is present, of course, but so are inertia and the allure of near-term gains and the preferences of the world's workers and consumers, who fall somewhere on a long spectrum of culpability stretching from knowing selfishness through true ignorance and reflexive, if naive, complacency. How do you spin that yarn?

When Bill McKibben declared *The End of Nature* in 1989, he was posing a hyperbolic kind of epistemological riddle: What do you call it, whatever *it* is, when forces of wilderness and weather, of animal kingdoms and plant life, have been so transformed by human activity that they are no longer truly "natural"?

The answer came a few decades later with the term "the

Anthropocene"—a name given to the geological era we live in now, where human activity is the dominant influence on the environment. The term was coined in the spirit of environmental alarm and suggested a much messier and more unstable state than "end." Environmentalists, outdoors people, nature lovers, and romantics of various stripes—there are many who would mourn the end of nature. But there are literally billions who will shortly be terrified by the forces unleashed by the Anthropocene. In much of the world, they already are, in the form of lethal close-to-annual heat waves in the Middle East and South Asia, and in the ever-present threat of floods, like those that hit the Indian state of Kerala in 2018 and killed hundreds. The floods hardly made a mark in the United States and Europe, where consumers of news have been trained over decades to see disasters like these as tragic, yes, but also as an inevitable feature of underdevelopment—and therefore both "natural" and distant.

The arrival of this scale of climate suffering in the modern West will be one of the great and terrible stories of the coming decades. There, at least, we've long thought that modernity had paved over nature, completely, factory by factory and strip mall by strip mall. Proponents of solar geoengineering want to take on the sky next, not just to stabilize the planet's temperature but possibly to create "designer climates," localized to very particular needs—saving this reef ecosystem, preserving that breadbasket. Conceivably those climates could get considerably more micro, down to particular farms or soccer stadiums or beach resorts.

These interventions, should they ever become feasible, are decades away, at least. But even rapid and quotidian-seeming projects will leave a profoundly different imprint on the shape of the world. In the nineteenth century, the built environment of the most advanced countries reflected the prerogatives of industry—think of railroad tracks laid across whole continents to move coal. In the twentieth century, those same environments were made to reflect the needs of capital—think of global urbanization agglomerating labor supply for a new service economy. In the twenty-first century, they will reflect the demands of the climate crisis: seawalls, carbon-capture plantations, state-size solar arrays. The claims of eminent domain made on behalf of climate change will no longer play like government overreach, though they will still surely inspire NIMBY backlash—even in a time of climate crisis, people will find ways to look out for number one.

We are already living within a deformed environment—indeed, quite deformed. In its swaggering twentieth century, the United States built two states of paradise: Florida, out of dismal swamp, and Southern California, out of desert. By 2100, neither will endure as Edenic postcards.

That we reengineered the natural world so sufficiently to close the book on an entire geological era—that is the major lesson of the Anthropocene. The scale of that transformation remains astonishing, even to those of us who were raised amidst it and took all its imperious values for granted. Twenty-two percent of the earth's landmass was altered by humans just between 1992 and 2015; 96 percent of the world's mammals, by weight, are now humans and their livestock; only 4 percent are wild. We have simply crowded—or bullied, or brutalized—every other species into retreat, near-extinction, or worse. E. O. Wilson thought the era might be better called the Eremocine—the age of loneliness.

But global warming carries a message more concerning still: we didn't defeat the environment at all. There was no final conquest, no dominion established. In fact, the opposite. Whatever it means for the other animals on the planet, with global warming we have unwittingly claimed ownership of a system beyond our ability to control or tame in any day-to-day way. And more than that: with our continued activity, we have rendered that system yet more out of control. Nature is both over, as in "past," and all around us, overwhelming us and punishing us—this is the major lesson of climate change, which it teaches us almost daily.

For decades now, there have been few things with a worse reputation than "alarmism" among scientists studying climate change. James Hansen, who first testified before Congress about global warming in 1988, has named the phenomenon "scientific reticence," and in 2007 chastised his colleagues for editing their own observations so conscientiously that they failed to communicate how dire the threat really was. Which is why scientific reticence is another reason we don't see the threat so clearly—the experts signaling strongly that it is irresponsible to communicate openly about the more worrisome possibilities for global warming, as though they didn't trust the world with the information they themselves had, or at least didn't trust the public to interpret it and respond properly. Whatever that means: it has now been thirty years since Hansen's first testimony and the establishment of the IPCC, and climate concern has traversed small peaks and small valleys but never meaningfully jumped upward. As for public response, the results are even more dismal. Within the United States, climate denial took over one of the two major parties and essentially vetoed major legislative action. Abroad, we have had a series of high-profile conferences, treaties, and accords, but they increasingly look like so many acts of climate kabuki. Emissions are still growing, unabated.

But scientific reticence is also perfectly reasonable. Scientists were especially worried about burnout, and the possibility that honest storytelling about climate could tip so many people into despondency that the effort to avert a crisis would burn itself out. And in generalizing from that experience, they pointed to a selection of social science suggesting that "hope" can be more motivating than "fear"—without acknowledging, however, that alarm is not the same as fatalism, that hope does not demand silence about scarier challenges, and that fear can motivate, too. That was the finding of a 2017 paper in *Nature* surveying the full breadth of the academic literature: despite a strong consensus among climate scientists about "hope" and "fear" and what qualifies as responsible storytelling, there is no single way to best tell the story of climate change, no single rhetorical approach likely to work on a given audience, and none too dangerous to try. Any story that sticks is a good one.

In 2018, scientists began embracing fear, when the IPCC

released a dramatic, alarmist report illustrating just how much worse climate change would be at 2 degrees of warming compared with 1.5: tens of millions more people exposed to deadly heat waves, water shortages, and flooding. The research summarized in the report was not new, and temperatures beyond 2 degrees were not even covered. But though it did not address any of the scarier possibilities for warming, the report did offer a new form of permission, of sanction, to the world's scientists. The thing that was new was the message: *It is okay, finally, to freak out.*

The Church of Technology

SHOULD ANYTHING SAVE US, IT WILL BE TECHNOLOGY. BUT within the futurist fraternity of Silicon Valley, technologists have little more than fairy tales to offer. Over the last decade, consumer adoration has anointed those founders and venture capitalists something like shamans, Ouija-boarding their way toward blueprints for the world's future. But conspicuously few of them seem meaningfully concerned about climate change. Instead, they make parsimonious investments in green energy (the examples of Elon Musk and Bill Gates aside) and fewer still philanthropic payouts (Bill Gates again aside).

The following encapsulates the prevailing mindset:

In "An Account of My Hut," a memoir of Bay Area househunting and climate-apocalypse-watching in the 2017 California wildfire season—which was also the season of Hurricanes Harvey and Irma and Maria—Christina Nichol describes a conversation with a young family member who works in tech, to whom she tried to describe the unprecedentedness of the threat from climate change, unsuccessfully. "Why worry?" he replies.

> "Technology will take care of everything. If the Earth goes, we'll just live in spaceships. We'll have 3D printers to print our food. We'll be eating lab meat. One cow will feed us all. We'll just rearrange atoms to create water or oxygen. Elon Musk."

> Elon Musk—it's not the name of a man but a species-scale survival strategy. Nichol answers, "But I don't *want* to live in a spaceship."

> "He looked genuinely surprised. In his line of work, he'd never met anyone who didn't want to live in a spaceship."

That technology might liberate us, collectively, from the strain of labor and material privation is a dream at least as old as John Maynard Keynes, who predicted his grandchildren would work only fifteen-hour weeks, and yet never be ultimately fulfilled. In 1987, the year he won the Nobel Prize, economist Robert Solow famously commented, "You can see the computer age everywhere but in the productivity statistics."

This has been, even more so, the experience of most of those living in the developed world in the decades since—rapid technological change transforming nearly every aspect of everyday life and yet yielding little or no tangible improvement in any conventional measures of economic well-being. It is probably one explanation for contemporary political discontent—a perception that the world is being almost entirely remade but in a way that leaves you, as delighted as you may be by Netflix and Amazon and Instagram and Google Maps, more or less exactly where you were before.

The same can be said, believe it or not, for the much-heralded green energy "revolution," which has yielded productivity gains in energy and cost reductions far beyond the predictions of even the most doe-eyed optimists, and yet has not even bent the curve of carbon emissions downward. We are, in other words, billions of dollars and thousands of dramatic breakthroughs later, precisely where we started when hippies were affixing solar panels to their geodesic domes. That is because the market has not responded to these developments by seamlessly retiring dirty energy sources and replacing them with clean ones. It has responded by simply adding the new capacity to the same system.

Over the last twenty-five years, the cost per unit of renewable energy has fallen so far that you can hardly measure the price, today, using the same scales (only since 2009, for instance, solar energy costs have fallen more than 80 percent). Over the same twenty-five years, the proportion of global energy use derived from renewables hasn't grown much. We are now burning 80 percent more coal than we were in the year 2000.

And energy is, actually, the least of it. As the futurist Alex Steffen has incisively put it, in a Twitter performance that functions as a "Powers of Ten" for the climate crisis, the transition from dirty electricity to clean sources is not the whole challenge. It's just the lowest-hanging fruit: "smaller than the challenge of electrifying almost everything that uses power," Steffen says, by which he means anything that runs on much dirtier gas engines. That task, he continues, is smaller than the challenge of reducing energy demand, which is smaller than the challenge of reinventing how goods and services are provided—given that global supply chains are built with dirty infrastructure and labor markets everywhere are still powered by dirty energy. There is also the need to get to zero emissions from all other sources—deforestation, agriculture, livestock, landfills. And the need to protect all human systems from the coming onslaught of natural disasters and extreme weather. And the need to erect a system of global government, or at least international cooperation, to coordinate such a project. All of which is a smaller task, Steffen says, "than the monumental cultural undertaking of imagining together a thriving, dynamic, sustainable future that feels not only possible, but worth fighting for."

On this last point I see things differently—the imagination isn't the hard part, especially for those less informed about the challenges than Steffen is. If we could wish a solution into place by imagination, we'd have solved the problem already. In fact, we *have* imagined the solutions; more than that, we've even developed them, at least in the form of green energy. We just haven't yet discovered the political will, economic might, and cultural flexibility to install and activate them, because doing so requires something a lot bigger and more concrete than imagination—it means nothing short of a complete overhaul of the world's energy systems, transportation, infrastructure, and industry and agriculture.

We think of climate change as slow, but it is unnervingly fast. We think of the technological change necessary to avert it as fast-arriving, but unfortunately it is deceptively slow—especially judged by just how soon we need it. This is what Bill McKibben means when he says that winning slowly is the same as losing: "If we don't act quickly, and on a global scale, then the problem will literally become insoluble," he writes. "The decisions we make in 2075 won't matter."

Innovation, in many cases, is the easy part. This is what the novelist William Gibson meant when he said, "The future is already here, it just isn't evenly distributed." Gadgets like the iPhone give a false picture of the pace of adaptation. To a wealthy American or Swede or Japanese, the market penetration may seem total, but more than a decade after its introduction, the device is used by less than 10 percent of the world; for all smartphones, even the "cheap" ones, the number is somewhere between a quarter and a third of the world. Define the technology in even more basic terms, as "cell phones" or "the internet," and you get a timeline to global saturation of at least decades—of which we have two or three in which to completely eliminate carbon emissions, planetwide. According to the IPCC, we have just twelve years to cut them in half. The longer we wait, the harder it will be. If we had started global decarbonization in 2000, when Al Gore narrowly lost election to the American presidency, we would have had to cut emissions by only about 3 percent per year to stay safely under two degrees of warming. If we start today, when global emissions are still growing, the necessary rate per year is 10 percent. If we delay another decade, it will require us to cut emissions by 30 percent each year. This is why UN Secretary-General António Guterres believes we have only one year to change course and get started.

The scale of the technological transformation required dwarfs any achievement that has emerged from Silicon Valley—in fact, it dwarfs every technological revolution ever engineered in human history, including electricity and telecommunications and even the invention of agriculture ten thousand years ago. It dwarfs them by definition, because it contains all of them—every single one needs to be replaced at the root, since every single one breathes on carbon, like a ventilator.

Thankfully, the green energy revolution is already, as they say, "under way." In fact, of all the necessary components of this broader, zero-carbon revolution, clean energy is probably farthest along. But even so, the gap between how fast we are moving and how fast we need to yawns so wide it could swallow whole civilizations, and indeed threatens to. Into it has crawled that dream of carbon capture: if we can't rebuild the entire infrastructure of the modern world in time to save it from self-destruction, perhaps we can at least buy ourselves some time by sucking some of its toxic fumes out of the air. Given the indomitable scale of the conventional approach, and given just how little time left we have to complete it, negative emissions may be, at present, a form of magical thinking for climate. They also seem like a last, best hope. And if they work, carbon capture plants will deliver industrial absolution for industrial sin—and initiate, as a result, a whole new theological romance with the power of machine.

It has been decades now since nuclear power was seen as a path to energy salvation rather than, as it still is so often today, through the specter of metaphysical contagion. And it has been at least a generation since the world stopped believing nuclear power was, in an environmental sense, "free" and started thinking of it in terms of nuclear war, meltdown, mutation, and cancer. That we remember the names of power-plant disasters is a sign of just how scarred we feel by them: Three Mile Island, Chernobyl, Fukushima.

But the scars are almost phantom ones, given the casualty numbers. The death toll of the incident at Three Mile Island is in some dispute, as many activists believe the true impact of radiation was suppressed—perhaps a reasonable belief, since the official account insists on no adverse health impacts at all. But the most pedigreed research suggests the meltdown increased cancer risk, within a ten-mile radius, by less than one-tenth of 1 percent. For Chernobyl, the official death count is 47, though some estimates run higher—even as high as 4,000. For Fukushima, according to a United Nations report, "no discernible increased incidence of radiation-related health effects are expected among exposed members of the public or their descendants." Had none of the 100,000 living in the evacuation zone ever left, perhaps a few hundred might have ultimately died of cancers related to the radiation.

Any number of dead is a tragedy, but more than 10,000 people die each day, globally, from the small-particulate pollution produced by burning carbon. This is not even broaching the subject of warming and its impacts. A rule change to pollution standards for coal producers, proposed by Trump's EPA in 2018, would kill an additional 1,400 Americans annually, the agency itself acknowledged; globally, pollution kills as many as 9 million people each year.

We live with that pollution, and with those death tolls, and hardly notice them; the curving concrete towers of nuclear plants, by contrast, stand astride the horizon like Chekhov's proverbial gun on the wall. Today, despite a variety of projects aimed at producing cheap nuclear energy, the price of new plants remains high enough that it is hard to make a persuasive argument that more green investment be directed toward them rather than installations of wind and solar. But the case for decommissioning and dismantling existing plants is considerably weaker, and yet that is exactly what is happening—from the United States, where both Three Mile Island and Indian Point are being closed down, to Germany, which retired its plants even more dramatically than it scaled up its state-of-the-world green energy program.

The contaminationist view of nuclear power is a misguided climate parable, arising nevertheless from a perceptive environmentalist perspective—that the healthy, clean natural world is made toxic by the intrusions and interventions of human industry. But the main lesson from the church of technology runs in the other direction, instructing us in subtle and not-so-subtle ways to regard the world beyond our phones as less real, less urgent, and less meaningful than the worlds made available to us through those screens, which happen to be worlds protected from climate devastation. As Andreas Malm has wondered, "How many will play augmented reality games on a planet that is six degrees warmer?" The poet and musician Kae Tempest puts it more brinily: "Staring into the screen so we don't have to see the planet die."

Politics of Consumption

IT IS A COMMON CHARGE AGAINST LIBERAL ENVIRONMENTALISTS THAT they live hypocritically—eating meat, flying, and voting liberal without yet having purchased Teslas. But among the woke left, the inverted charge is just as often true: we navigate by a North Star of politics through our diets, our friendships, even our consumption of pop culture, but rarely make meaningful political noise about those causes that run against our own self-interest or sense of self as special—indeed enlightened. And so, in the coming years, divestment is likely to be just the first salvo in a moral arms race between universities, municipalities, and nations. Cities will compete to be the first to ban cars, to paint every single roof white, to produce all the agriculture eaten by residents in vertical farms that don't require post-harvest transportation by automobile, railroad, or airplane. But liberal NIMBYism will still strut, too, as it did in 2018, when American voters in deep-blue Washington

State rejected a carbon tax at the ballot box, and the worst French protests since the quasi-revolution of 1968 raged against a proposed gasoline tax. On perhaps no issue more than climate is that liberal posture of well-off enlightenment a defensive gesture: almost regardless of your politics or your consumption choices, the wealthier you are, the larger your carbon footprint.

But when critics of Al Gore compare his electricity use to that of the average Ugandan, they are not ultimately highlighting conspicuous and hypocritical personal consumption, however they mean to disparage him. Instead, they are calling attention to the structure of a political and economic order that not only permits that disparity but feeds and profits from it—this is what Thomas Piketty calls the "apparatus of justification." And it justifies quite a lot. If the world's most conspicuous emitters, the top 10 percent, reduced their emissions to only the EU average, total global emissions would fall by 35 percent. We won't get there through the dietary choices of individuals but through policy changes. In an age of personal politics, hypocrisy can look like a cardinal sin; but it can also articulate a public aspiration. Eating organic is nice, in other words, but if your goal is to save the climate, your vote is much more important. Politics is a moral multiplier. And a perception of worldly sickness uncomplemented by political commitment gives us only "wellness."

It can be hard to take wellness seriously as a movement, at first, which may be why it has been the subject of so much derision over the past few years—SoulCycle, Goop, Moon Juice. But however manipulated by marketing consultants, and however dubious its claims to healthfulness, wellness also gives a clear name and shape to a growing perception even, or especially, among those wealthy enough to be insulated from the early assaults of climate change: that the contemporary world is toxic, and that to endure or thrive within it requires extraordinary measures of self-regulation and self-purification.

What has been called the "new New Age" arises from a similar intuition—that meditation, ayahuasca trips, crystals and Burning Man and microdosed LSD are all pathways to a world beckoning as purer, cleaner, more sustaining, and perhaps above all else, more whole. This purity arena is likely to expand, perhaps dramatically, as the climate continues to career toward visible degradation—and consumers respond by trying to extract themselves from the sludge of the world however they can. It should not be a surprise to discover, in next year's supermarket aisles, alongside labels for "organic" and "free range," some food described as "carbon-free." GMOs aren't a sign of a sick planet but a possible partial solution to the coming crisis of agriculture, as nuclear power may be for energy. But both have already become nearly as off-putting as carcinogens to the purity-minded, who are growing in number and channeling more and more ecological anxiety along the way.

That anxiety is coherent, even rational, at a time when it has been revealed that many American brand-name foods made from oats, including Cheerios and Quaker Oats, contain the pesticide

Roundup, which has been linked with cancer, and when the National Weather Service issues elaborate guidance about which commonly available face masks can, and which cannot, protect you against the wildfire smoke engulfing nearly all of North America. It is only intuitive, in other words, that impulses toward purity represent growth areas of our culture, destined to distend further inward from the cultural periphery as apocalyptic ecological anxiety grows, too.

But conscious consumption and wellness are both cop-outs, arising from that basic promise extended by neoliberalism: that consumer choices can be a substitute for political action, advertising not just political identity but political virtue; that the mutual end-goal of market and political forces should be the effective retirement of contentious politics at the hand of market consensus, which would displace ideological dispute; and that, in the meantime, in the supermarket aisle or department store, one can do good for the world simply by buying well.

It's fair to say that we already have at least two planetary dictators in the shape of mafia bosses, and global governance not on the do-gooder model but as a straight-up protection racket, and both are imperfect avatars of the archetype: Xi Jinping and Vladimir Putin, neither of whom is anti-capitalist so much as state capitalist. They also hold very different perspectives on the climate future and how to reckon with it, which suggests another variable, beyond form of government: climate ideology.

Their ideological contrast is clear. Putin, the commandant of a petro-state that also happens to be, given its geography, one of the few nations on Earth likely to benefit from continued warming, sees basically no benefit to constraining carbon emissions or greening the economy—Russia's or the world's. Xi, now the leader-for-life of the planet's rising superpower, seems to feel mutual obligations to the country's growing prosperity and to the health and security of its people—of whom, it's worth remembering, it has so many.

For decades, the rise of China has been an anxious prophecy invoked so regularly and so prematurely that Westerners, Americans especially, could be forgiven for thinking it was a case of the empire that cried wolf—an expression of Western self-doubt, more a premonition of collapse than a well-founded prediction of what new power might arise, and when. But on the matter of climate change, China does hold the cards. To the extent the world as a whole needs a stable climate to endure or thrive, its fate will be determined much more by the carbon trajectories of the developing world than by the course of the United States and Europe, where emissions have already flattened out and will likely begin their decline soon—though how dramatic a decline, and how soon, is very much up in the air. And although "carbon outsourcing" means that a significant slice of China's emissions is produced by manufacturing goods to be consumed by Americans and Europeans. Whose responsibility are those gigatons of carbon? It may not much longer be merely a rhetorical question if the Paris Accords yield to a more rigorous global carbon governance structure, as they were intended to, and add, along the way, a proper enforcement mechanism, military or otherwise. Already, French president Emmanuel Macron has threatened to spike a trade deal over Brazil's climate behavior, and promised not to enter into any new trade deal with a nation that was not honoring the Paris Accords (apparently unaware that France wasn't honoring them, either). And economists have begun to talk about a "Climate WTO," which would allow "virtuous" countries to reward one another and to punish climate laggards with sanctions—hoping, and it is always merely hoping with sanctions, that the tough line would bring about change.

All these scenarios, even the bleakest, presume some new political equilibrium. There is also, of course, the possibility of disequilibrium—or what you would normally call "disorder" and "conflict." This is the analysis put forward by Harald Welzer, in *Climate Wars,* which predicts a "renaissance" of violent conflict in the decades to come. His evocative subtitle: *What People Will Be Killed For in the 21st Century.*

Already, in local spheres, political collapse is a quite common outcome of climate crisis—we just call it civil war. And we tend to analyze it ideologically—as we did in Darfur, in Syria, in Yemen. Those kinds of collapses are likely to remain technically "local" rather than truly "global," though in a time of climate crisis, they would have an easier time metastasizing beyond old borders than they have in the recent past. In other words, a completely *Mad Max* world is not around the bend, since even catastrophic climate change won't undermine all political power—in fact, it will produce some winners, relatively speaking. Some of them with quite large armies and rapidly expanding surveillance states—China now pulls criminals out of pop concerts with facial recognition software and deploys domestic-spy drones indistinguishable from birds. This is not an aspiring empire likely to tolerate no-man's-lands within its sphere.

Mad Max regions elsewhere are another matter. In certain ways they are already here, where "here" is parts of Somalia or Iraq or South Sudan at various points in the last decade, including points when the planet's geopolitics seemed, at a glance from Los Angeles or London, stable. The idea of a "global order" has always been something of a fiction, or at least an aspiration, even as the joined forces of liberal internationalism, globalization, and American hegemony inched us toward it over the last century. Very probably, over the next century, climate change will reverse that course.

History After Progress

IF YOU STRIP THE PERCEPTION OF PROGRESS FROM HISTORY, what is left?

From here, it is hard, if not impossible, to see clearly what will emerge from the clouds of uncertainty around global warming—what forms we allow climate change to take, let alone what those forms will do to us. But it will not take a worst-case warming to deliver ravages dramatic enough to shake the casual sense that as time marches forward, life improves inevitably. Those ravages are likely to begin arriving quickly: new coastlines retreated from drowned cities; destabilized societies disgorging millions of refugees into neighboring ones already feeling the pinch of resource depletion; the last several hundred years, which many in the West saw as a simple line of progress and growing prosperity, rendered instead as a prelude to mass climate suffering. Exactly how we regard the shape of history in a time of climate change will be shaped by how much we do to avert that change and how much we let it remodel everything about our lives.

Climate change has been described as a revenge of time. "Man-made weather is never made in the present," Andreas Malm writes in *The Progress of This Storm,* his powerful sketch of a political theory for a time of climate change. "Global warming is a result of actions in the past."

It's a tidy formulation, one that vividly illustrates both the scale and the scope of the problem, which appears as the product of several long centuries of carbon-burning that also produced most of what we think of today as the comforting features of modern life. In that way, climate change does make us all prisoners of the Industrial Revolution and suggests a carceral model of history— progress arrested by the consequences of past behavior. But while the climate crisis was engineered in the past, it was mostly in the recent past; and the degree to which it transforms the world of our grandchildren is being decided not in nineteenth-century Manchester but today and in the decades ahead.

Disorientingly, climate change will also send us hurtling forward into an uncharted future—so long forward, if it proceeds unchecked, and into such a distant future that we can hardly imagine the scale. This is not the "techno-shock" first experienced by Victorians encountering an accelerating pace of progress and feeling overwhelmed by just how much was changing within a single lifetime—though we are now acquainting ourselves with that kind of change as well. It is more like the overwhelming awe felt by those naturalists contemplating the ancient-beyond-ancient historical grandeur of the earth, and calling it deep time.

But climate change inverts the perspective—giving us not a deep time of permanence but a deep time of cascading, disorienting change, so deep that it mocks any pretense of permanence on the planet. Pleasure districts like Miami Beach, built just decades ago, will disappear, as will many of the military installations erected around the world since World War II to defend and secure the wealth that gave rise to them. Much older cities, like Amsterdam, are also under threat from flooding, with extraordinary infrastructure already needed today to keep them above water, infrastructure unavailable to defend the temples and villages of Bangladesh. Farmlands that had produced the same strains of grain or grapes for centuries or more will adapt, if they are lucky, to entirely new crops; in Sicily, the breadbasket of the ancient world, farmers are already turning to tropical fruits. Arctic ice that formed over millions of years will be unleashed as water, literally changing the face of the planet and remodeling shipping routes responsible for the very idea of globalization. And mass migrations will sever communities numbering in the millions—even tens of millions—from their ancestral homelands, which will disappear forever.

Just how long the ecosystems of Earth will be thrown into flux and disarray from anthropogenic climate change also depends on how much more of that change we choose to engineer—and perhaps how much we can manage to undo. But warming at the level necessary to fully melt ice sheets and glaciers and elevate sea level by several hundred feet promises to initiate rolling, radically transformative changes on a timescale measured not in decades or centuries or even millennia, but in the millions of years. Alongside that timeline, the entire life span of human civilization is rendered, effectively, an afterthought; and the much longer span of climate change becomes eternity.

Ethics at the End of the World

IN THE UNITED STATES, THOSE CALLING FOR MASS MOBILIZA-
tion, starting today and no later, and thrillingly inspiring millions
around the world to march and protest and demand the same—
these can be counted as environmental pragmatists. To their left
are those who see no solution short of political revolution. And
even those activists are being crowded for space by texts of climate alarmism, of which you may feel the book in your hands is
one. That would be fair enough, because I am alarmed.

I am not alone. And how widespread alarm will shape our
ethical impulses toward one another, and the politics that emerge
from those impulses, is among the more profound questions
being posed by the climate to the planet of people it envelops.
You can't halfway your way to a solution to a crisis this large.

In the meantime, environmental panic is growing, and so is

despair. Over the last several years, as unprecedented weather and unrelenting research have recruited more voices to the army of environmental panic, a dour terminological competition has sprung up among climate writers, aiming to coin new clarifying language—in the mode of Richard Heinberg's "toxic knowledge" or Kris Bartkus's "Malthusian tragic"—to give epistemological shape to the demoralizing, or demoralized, response of the rest of the world. To the environmental indifference expected of modern consumers, the philosopher and activist Wendy Lynne Lee has given the name "eco-nihilism." British Columbian Stuart Parker's "climate nihilism" is easier on the tongue. Bruno Latour, an instinctive insubordinate, calls the menace of a raging environment fueled by indifferent politics a "climatic regime." We have also "climate fatalism" and "ecocide" and what Sam Kriss and Ellie Mae O'Hagan, making a psychoanalytic argument against the relentless public-facing optimism of environmental advocacy, have called "human futilitarianism."

The novelist Richard Powers points his finger at a different kind of despair, "species loneliness," which he identifies not as the impression left on us by environmental degradation but what has inspired us, seeing the imprint we are leaving, to nevertheless continue pressing onward: "the sense we're here by ourselves, and there can be no purposeful act except to gratify ourselves." As though initiating a more accommodationist wing of Dark Mountain, he suggests a retreat from anthropocentrism that is not quite a withdrawal from modern civilization: "We have to un-blind ourselves to human exceptionalism. That's the real challenge. Unless forest-health is our health, we're never going to get beyond appetite as a motivator in the world. The exciting challenge," he says, is to make people "plant-conscious."

Gazing out at the future from the promontory of the present, with the planet having warmed one degree, the world of two degrees seems nightmarish—and the worlds of three degrees, and four, yet more grotesque. But one way we might manage to navigate that path without crumbling collectively in despair is, perversely, to normalize climate suffering at the same pace we accelerate it, as we have so much human pain over centuries, so that we are always coming to terms with what is just ahead of us, decrying what lies beyond that, and forgetting all that we had ever said about the absolute moral unacceptability of the conditions of the world we are passing through in the present tense, and blithely.

IV

THE ANTHROPIC PRINCIPLE

NO ONE WANTS TO SEE DISASTER COMING, BUT THOSE WHO look, do. Climate science has arrived at this terrifying conclusion not casually, and not with glee, but by systematically ruling out every alternative explanation for observed warming—even though that observed warming is more or less precisely what would be expected given only the rudimentary understanding of the greenhouse effect advanced by John Tyndall and Eunice Foote in the 1850s, when America was reaching its first industrial peak. What we are left with is a set of predictions that can appear falsifiable—about global temperatures, sea-level rise, and even hurricane frequency and wildfire volume. But, all told, the question of how bad things will get is not actually a test of the science; it is a bet on human activity. How much will we do to stall disaster, and how quickly?

Those are the only questions that matter. There are, it is true, feedback loops we don't understand and dynamic warming processes scientists haven't yet pinpointed. Yet to the extent we live today under clouds of uncertainty about climate change, those clouds are projections not of collective ignorance about the natural world but blindness about the human one, and can be dispersed by human action. This is what it means to live beyond the "end of nature"— it is human action that will determine the climate of the future, not systems beyond our control. If we allow global warming to proceed, and to punish us with all the ferocity we have fed it, it will be because we have chosen that punishment, collectively walking down a path of suicide. If we avert it, it will be because we have chosen to walk a different path, and to endure.

These are the disconcerting, contradictory lessons of global warming, which counsels both human humility and human grandiosity, each drawn from the same perception of peril. The climate system that gave rise to the human species, and to everything we know of as civilization, is so fragile that it has been brought to the brink of total instability by just one generation of human activity. But that instability is also a measure of the human power that engineered it, almost by accident, and which now must stop the damage, in only as much time. If humans are responsible for the problem, they must be capable of undoing it. We have an idiomatic name for those who hold the fate of the world in their hands, as we do: gods. But for the moment at least, most of us seem more inclined to run from that responsibility than embrace it—or even to admit we see it, though it sits in front of us as plainly as a steering wheel.

Instead, we assign the task to future generations, to dreams of magical technologies, to remote politicians doing a kind of battle with profiteering delay. This is why this book is also studded so oppressively with "we," however imperious it may seem. The fact that climate change is all-enveloping means it targets all of us, and we must all share in the responsibility so we do not all share in the suffering—at least not all share in so suffocatingly much of it.

We do not know the precise shape such suffering would take, cannot predict with certainty exactly how many acres of forest will burn each year of the next century, releasing into the air centuries of stored carbon; or how many hurricanes will flatten each Caribbean island; or where megadroughts are likely to produce mass famines first; or which will be the first great pandemic to be produced by global warming. But we know enough to see, even now, that the new world we are stepping into will be so alien from our own, it might as well be another planet entirely.

The threat from climate change is more total than from the atomic bomb. It is also more pervasive. In a 2018 paper, forty-two scientists from around the world warned that, in an unabated-emissions scenario, no ecosystem on Earth was safe, with transformation "ubiquitous and dramatic," exceeding in just one or two centuries the amount of change that unfolded in the most dramatic periods of transformation in the earth's history over tens of thousands of years. Half of the Great Barrier Reef has already died, methane is leaking from Arctic permafrost that may never freeze again, and the high-end estimates for what warming will mean for cereal crops suggest that just four degrees of warming could reduce yields by 50 percent. If this strikes you as tragic, which it should, consider that we have all the tools we need, today, to stop it all: a carbon tax and the political apparatus to aggressively phase out dirty energy; a new approach to agricultural practices and a shift away from beef and dairy in the global diet; and public investment in green energy and carbon capture.

That the solutions are obvious, and available, does not mean the problem is anything but overwhelming. It is not a subject that can sustain only one narrative, one perspective, one metaphor, one mood. This will become only more so in the coming decades, as the signature of global warming appears on more and more disasters, political horrors, and humanitarian crises. There will be those, as there are now, who rage against fossil capitalists and their political enablers, and others, as there are now, who lament human shortsightedness and decry the consumer excesses of contemporary life. There will be those, as there are now, who fight as unrelenting activists, with approaches as diverse as federal lawsuits and aggressive legislation and small-scale protests of new pipelines; nonviolent resistance; and civil-rights crusades. And there will be those, as there are now, who see the cascading suffering and fall back into an inconsolable despair. There will be those, as there are now, who insist that there is only one way to respond to the unfolding ecological catastrophe—one productive way, one responsible way.

Presumably, it won't be only one way. Even before the age of climate change, the literature of conservation furnished many metaphors to choose from. James Lovelock gave us the Gaia hypothesis, which conjured an image of the world as a single, evolving quasi-biological entity. Buckminster Fuller popularized "spaceship earth," which presents the planet as a kind of desperate life raft in what American poet and playwright Archibald MacLeish called "the enormous, empty night"; today, the phrase suggests a vivid picture of a world spinning through the solar system barnacled with enough carbon capture plants to actually stall out warming, or even reverse it, restoring as if by magic the breathability of the air between the machines. The *Voyager 1* space probe gave us the "Pale Blue Dot"—the inescapable smallness, and fragility, of the entire experiment we're engaged in, together, whether we like it or not. Personally, I think climate change itself offers the most invigorating picture, in that even its cruelty flatters our sense of power and, in so doing, calls the world as one to action. At least I hope it does. But that is another meaning of the climate kaleidoscope. You can choose your metaphor. You can't choose the planet, which is the only one any of us will ever call home.

Afterword

The final page of the manuscript of this book was written in early September of 2018, in a spirit of halfway optimism which, at the time, I halfway believed.

I knew enough to know that very few casual presumptions about the solubility of the climate crisis could survive a real encounter with its unmitigated brutality. And yet I rhapsodized still—about the dream of a genuinely inclusive, global, even universal perspective on the fate of the planet and those who hope to live on it. And earnestly invoked the possibility that, if we chose to see the climate that way, we could still secure a livable, fulfilling, just, and prosperous future for the world—at least relatively livable, relatively fulfilling, relatively just, and relatively prosperous, since we are already living on a planet gnawed by climate change and already see how easily intuitions of resource scarcity come to justify resource jealousy and, in the name of those privileged with comfort and security, excuse the disproportionate suffering of those most in need. Of course, that happier future is possible; the only thing standing in the way is ourselves and the obstacles we've erected everywhere, so that we must stumble forward over them to make any progress at all. The question is how much stock to put in our chances—chances that seemed, for decades, to narrow by the day, crowded out by carbon concentrations and toxic particulate matter like gas filling a room. Our only room.

Over the last year, the march of science has continued, its drumbeat just as dour, or more so: glaciers melting faster and permafrost, too; new record heat waves, new record wildfires, credible reports that a million distinct species could be on the verge of extinction; scientists raising the possibility, with new models, that anticipated emissions could produce significantly more warming this century than previously understood, and that, as early as next century, the planet could lose its capacity to produce clouds, which could alone add eight degrees of warming to our total. It may be fatalistic to wonder whether five degrees would bring about the collapse of civilization, or something close to it; it is foolish not to wonder the same about thirteen degrees.

The United Nations released its landmark "Doomsday" report in the fall of 2018, outlining in the starkest terms what unchecked global warming promised in the next decades, and just what scale of concerted, coordinated action was required to check it—a World War II–scale mobilization, the report said, in language dramatically more alarmist and urgent than anything produced by a similar body before. That mobilization would need to start, the secretary-general warned, within months. At the time, Greta Thunberg was an unknown Swedish schoolgirl who'd been quietly ditching every Friday to protest her country's inaction on climate change; over the next few months, she became the closest thing the climate movement has to a Joan of Arc, speaking with brutal honesty before the United Nations and the World Economic Forum and inspiring millions across Europe and the rest of the world to walk out, too. In the United Kingdom that same fall, the alarmist activist group Extinction Rebellion announced itself by commandeering five bridges in central London; their first demand was simply "Tell the truth." In the United States, the story was the same: the Sunrise Movement stormed the office of House Speaker-to-be Nancy Pelosi and, with the help of newly elected climate hero Alexandria Ocasio-Cortez, forced the Green New Deal into the very center of American political debate—an unprecedented leap from the political record of the Obama years, when many Democrats considered a modest cap-and-trade program too radical.

Opinion surveys were eye-opening. More Americans believed in climate change than ever before, more were worried about it, and more were alarmed by it—in fact, in an ironic reflection of disinformation campaigns, more Americans told pollsters they were anxious about global warming than believed there was overwhelming scientific consensus about it. In some cases, the numbers tracking concern had jumped ten points in a single year.

Of course, the world's levers of power are not pulled directly by public opinion, and when they are pulled by it, the pull tends to be long and slow. Even among environmentalists, there were those who wondered just how serious the protestors were—arguing over the place of nuclear power or the wisdom of linking a climate agenda with a social-justice one—and, remembering the earlier, smaller burst of concern around the time of Hurricane Katrina and *An Inconvenient Truth*, just how long it all would last.

Incredibly, the climate protests of the last year have already produced much more than simple shifts in public mood. Early in 2019, Greta secured a commitment from the president of the European Union that fully a quarter of all EU spending would be directed at climate adaptation and mitigation; she had just turned sixteen. By the summer, Extinction Rebellion had helped pressure British Parliament to declare a climate emergency—a Parliament under conservative control and consumed by the specter and politics of Brexit. On her way out the door, Theresa May committed the country to carbon neutrality by 2050. Her successor, Boris Johnson, promised a ban on the sale of all non-electric cars by 2030.

Each of these pledges was categorically more serious and ambitious than anything considered politically feasible—or even dreamable—as recently as a few months before. But to trust the cautious judgment of the United Nations, which insisted we had barely a decade to halve emissions, they were also hopelessly inadequate to the task of avoiding climate catastrophe. In the case of Britain, suddenly a rival to Germany for the crown of global renewable leader, it was also less than might be credibly demanded of a nation burdened by so much historical carbon guilt—though of course it was miles better than the United States, whose historical emissions dwarfed Britain's. But if a skeptic could be forgiven for doubting the power of widespread protest, a climate optimist could be forgiven for thinking something like the opposite: that everything was moving in the right direction except time, of which we have so little.

And yet, with climate as with everything else, history does not move in a straight line. In the United States, Michael Bloomberg pledged $500 million to force the retirement of American coal, while in China investment in renewable energy collapsed in the first half of 2019—a pattern followed, terrifyingly, by the rest of the world as well. American oil companies lobbied for a carbon tax, but asked, in return, for a moratorium on future climate liability lawsuits, and in June those Democratic candidates for the presidency, who'd seen global warming rise improbably to the top shelf of voter concerns, were told by their party that there would be no climate debate. That same month, Canada declared a climate emergency and then, the very next day, approved a new oil pipeline. In the aftermath of the murder of journalist Jamal Khashoggi on his watch, Mohammed bin Salman, the would-be ruler of Saudi Arabia, mused about the need for his country's economy to leave behind the production of fossil fuels, then months later began exploring once again the possibility of an IPO for Aramco, the national oil company, and was awarded the next G20 conference. *The New York Times* revealed that the work of climate skepticism carried out by the Competitive Enterprise

Institute, a leading libertarian think tank, was done with the support of "major corporations, like Google and Amazon, that have made their commitment to addressing climate change a key part of their corporate public relations strategies."

I have written, forgivingly, about a different kind of perceived climate hypocrisy—those who call for change while still flying and eating hamburgers, who probably perceive that politics does offer a more productive path than lifestyle choices, which even multiplied across like-minded communities would have only small or intermediary impacts. But the growing hypocrisy of the truly empowered—corporations, nations, political leaders— illustrates a far more concerning possibility, all the more alarming for being so familiar from other realms of politics: that climate talk could become not a spur to change but an alibi, a cover, for inaction and irresponsibility, the world's most powerful uniting in a chorus of double-talk that produces little beyond the song.

Meanwhile, the less powerful will simply have to get used to it—almost invariably, the least powerful having to adjust to the most. This is the real menace of the calm-sounding term "normalization," which threatens to describe the brutal readjustment to the lives of many billions of the world's poorest nations, which have already, according to one study, lost a quarter of potential GDP growth over recent decades thanks to climate change. But normalization will also infect the lives of the world's well-off, who will no longer be as protected from the forces of nature as they fancied themselves to be in decades past, as I saw vividly in the spring of 2019, when I traveled to California to take a peek at the future of wildfire.

When I arrived in Los Angeles in March 2019, it was on the thirty-first consecutive day of rain. This was an epic deluge for a drought-stricken state, but it was also a mixed blessing, as not only fire scientists but firefighters and local politicians and some exceptionally well informed Californians told me. In the state's forests, drought and heat reliably create fire conditions—they are the main reasons that climate change promises longer and probably more intense burn seasons in the future. The drought that lasted from 2010 to 2016, for instance, left behind 147 million dead trees; today, according to Cal Fire, there are 357 million. But in greater Los Angeles, the better predictor is actually the availability of grassland, which grows more bountifully when it rains. This sequence of extreme weather may sound paradoxical—historic rains followed quickly by fear of fire—but climate change promises to make everything more extreme, including sudden meteorological reversals. Los Angeles can seem, in this way, ahead of its time, a preview of the climate future the rest of the world is only peeking at through stretched fingers: communities across the city contemplating the terrifying impacts to come and wondering just how comfortable, or even manageable, life under those conditions could possibly be.

Instead, what I found there was a very different kind of

preview of the warming future—a case study in normalization, whereby we reflexively recalibrate our expectations so that we are never as shocked or horrified as we should be by the suffering we are living through today and expecting to arrive tomorrow. California has a long history with wildfire, which offers a long syllabus for normalization, and while nearly everyone I spoke with had registered the last two fire seasons as exceptional—even as horror shows—it seemed only to have bound them more deeply to the same volatile, punishing land. I met a woman who'd made her home in Malibu long enough to live through nine fires and was considering moving only now, she said, for personal reasons. I spoke to a surfer who complained that for months last winter the water smelled like fire and tasted like ash, but kept surfing. I talked to several people who refused mandatory evacuations. None of them planned to honor them the next time, either, when an evacuation bullhorn might wake them at 2:00 a.m., the monstrous fire sparked only since they went to sleep.

These were just anecdotes from civilians, but the politics of fire in California, where firefighters have never once stopped a blaze powered by Santa Ana winds, reflect a similar spirit of disturbing reorientation. California fires are five times larger than they were in the 1970s, with summertime fires eight times bigger; and conservative estimates suggest that as soon as 2050, the area burned each year by forest fires across the western United States will at least double, and perhaps quadruple. That is slightly less than three decades from now—the length of the mortgages that banks have extended to the homes on those fire-prone lands. After that, the picture becomes murkier—projections diverge, mid-century, in part because different scientists take different approaches to estimating just what the fire environment will look like in a particular ecosystem once all its land has burned. In greater Los Angeles, that could happen by 2050, when past experience, harrowing and biblical as it may seem, could cease to be any kind of guide for what's ahead. "There's no number of helicopters or trucks that we can buy, no number of firefighters that we can have, no amount of brush that we can clear that will stop this," former mayor Eric Garcetti told me. "The only thing that will stop this is when the Earth, probably long after we're gone, relaxes into a more predictable weather state."

Until then, unless we take dramatic action and reshape the whole conglomerated machine of modern life away from carbon, we may comfort ourselves, perversely, by remembering that the world has always had droughts and floods and hurricanes, heat waves and famines and war. And will likely fall into spasms of panic—some of us, sometimes—considering that a future of so many more of them seems so unlivable, unconscionable, even uncontemplable today. In between, we will go about our daily business as though the crisis were not so present, enduring in a world increasingly defined by the brutality of climate change through compartmentalization and denial, by lamenting our burned-over politics and our incinerated sense of the future but only rarely connecting them to the baking of the planet, and now and again by making some progress, then patting ourselves on the back for it, though it was never enough progress, and never in time.

Punishments from warming are already unequal, and presumably will grow more so—within communities, within nations, and globally. Those with power to make meaningful change are often those today most protected from warming; in many cases, they are the ones who stand to benefit, typically handsomely, from inaction. And yet climate change is also, inarguably, a saga in which we are all implicated and which threatens to deform all our lives should we not change course. The solutions, when we dare to imagine them, are global as well, which makes universal language, I think, even if not precisely accurate, nevertheless fitting and illustrative, and indeed motivating, if there is to be any chance of preserving even the hope for that happier future—relatively livable, relatively fulfilling, relatively prosperous, and perhaps more than relatively just. Call me crazy or better yet naive, but I still think we can.

Acknowledgments

If this book is worth anything, it is worth that because of the work of the scientists who first theorized, then documented the warming of the planet, and then began examining and explicating what that warming might mean for the rest of us living on it. That line of debt runs from Eunice Foote and John Tyndall in the nineteenth century to Roger Revelle and Charles David Keeling in the twentieth and on to all of those hundreds of scientists whose labor has inspired and helped me with this book (and of course many hundreds of unmentioned others very hard at work). However much progress we manage against the assaults of climate change in the coming decades, it is thanks to them.

I am personally indebted to those scientists, climate writers, and activists who were especially generous to me, over the last several years, with their time and insights—helping me understand their own research and pointing me to the findings of others, indulging my requests for rambling interviews or discussing the state of the planet with me in other public settings, corresponding with me over time, and, in many cases, reviewing my writing, including portions of the text of this book, before publication. They are Richard Alley, David Archer, Craig Baker-

Austin, David Battisti, Peter Brannen, Wallace Smith Broecker, Marshall Burke, Ethan D. Coffel, Aiguo Dai, Peter Gleick, Jeff Goodell, Al Gore, James Hansen, Katharine Hayhoe, Geoffrey Heal, Solomon Hsiang, Matthew Huber, Nancy Knowlton, Robert Kopp, Lee Kump, Irakli Loladze, Charles Mann, Geoff Mann, Michael Mann, Kate Marvel, Bill McKibben, Michael Oppenheimer, Naomi Oreskes, Andrew Revkin, Joseph Romm, Lynn Scarlett, Steven Sherwood, Joel Wainwright, Peter D. Ward, and Elizabeth Wolkovich.

When I first wrote about climate change in 2017, I relied also on the critical research help of Julia Mead and Ted Hart. I am grateful, too, to all the responses to that story that were published elsewhere—especially those by Genevieve Guenther, Eric Holthaus, Farhad Manjoo, Susan Mathews, Jason Mark, Robinson Meyer, Chris Mooney, and David Roberts. That includes all the scientists who reviewed my work for the website Climate Feedback, working through my story line by line. In preparing this manuscript for publication, Chelsea Leu reviewed it even more closely, and incisively, and I cannot thank her enough for that.

This book would not have come to be without the vision, guidance, wisdom, and forbearance of Tina Bennett, to whom I now owe a lifetime of thanks. And it would not have become an actual book without the acuity, brilliance, and faith of Tim Duggan, and the enormously helpful work of William Wolfslau and Molly Stern, Dyana Messina, Julia Bradshaw, Christine Johnson, Aubrey Martinson, Julie Cepler, Rachel Aldrich, Craig

Adams, Phil Leung, and Andrea Lau, Svetlana Katz and Laura Bonner, as well as Helen Conford and Laura Stickney, Isabel Blake, Holly Hunter, Ingrid Matts, and Will O'Mullane.

I would not be writing this book were it not for Central Park East, and especially Pam Cushing, my second mother. I'm grateful to everyone I work with at *New York* magazine for all of their encouragement and support along the way. This goes especially for my bosses Jared Hohlt, Adam Moss, and Pam Wasserstein, and David Haskell, my editor and friend and co-conspirator. Other friends and co-conspirators also helped refine and reconceive what it was I was trying to do in this book, and to all of them I am so thankful, too: Isaac Chotiner, Kerry Howley, Hua Hsu, Christian Lorentzen, Noreen Malone, Chris Parris-Lamb, Willa Paskin, Max Read, and Kevin Roose. For a million unenumerable things, I'd also like to thank Jerry Saltz and Will Leitch, Lisa Miller and Vanessa Grigoriadis, Mike Marino and Andy Roth and Ryan Langer, James Darnton and Andrew Smeall and Scarlet Kim and Ann Fabian, Casey Schwartz and Marie Brenner, Nick Zimmerman and Dan Weber and Whitney Schubert and Joey Frank, Justin Pattner and Daniel Brand, Caitlin Roper, Ann Clarke and Alexis Swerdloff, Stella Bugbee, Meghan O'Rourke, Robert Asahina, Philip Gourevitch, Lorin Stein, and Michael Grunwald.

My best reader, as always, is my brother, Ben; without his footsteps to follow, who knows where I'd be. I've been inspired, too, in countless ways, by Harry and Roseann, Jenn and Matt and Heather, and above all by my mother and father, only one of whom is here to read this book but to both of whom I owe it, and everything else.

The last and biggest thanks belong to Risa, my love, and to Rocca, my other love—for the last year, the last twenty, and the fifty or more to come. Let's hope they're cool ones.

Index

About the Author

DAVID WALLACE-WELLS is a national fellow at the New America foundation and a columnist and deputy editor at *New York* magazine. He was previously the deputy editor of the *Paris Review*. He lives in New York City.

 @dwallace wells